Trash TO TREASURE

Making something from nothing gives us such a thrill, especially when we know we're helping save our environment. And it's fun, too! In fact, this newest idea-packed volume of Trash to Treasure *makes it easier than ever to reclaim our Earth's resources while creating nifty gifts and distinctive items for home decor. We've organized over seven dozen projects featuring common castoffs we all have at home. For instance, you'll see how super-simple it is to transform odd socks into terrific toys or to fashion empty cans into fabulous lamps. How about that empty beverage bottle? With just a little know-how, it's actually a clever candlestick. Take another look at that cardboard box to see the beginnings of a great little storage system — or a wonderful clock! You'll even find exciting new things to do with greeting cards and ordinary brown paper bags. With so many designs from which to choose, you won't have to stop after just one earth-friendly project . . . you can make them all!*

Anne Childs

LEISURE ARTS, INC.
Little Rock, Arkansas

EDITORIAL STAFF

EDITORIAL STAFF
Vice President and Editor-in-Chief:
Anne Van Wagner Childs
Executive Director: Sandra Graham Case
Design Director: Patricia Wallenfang Sowers
Editorial Director: Susan Frantz Wiles
Publications Director: Kristine Anderson Mertes
Creative Art Director: Gloria Bearden

DESIGN
Senior Designers: Polly Tullis Browning, Sandra Spotts Ritchie, and Billie Steward
Designers: Diana Sanders Cates, Cherece Athy Cooper, Cyndi Hansen, Dani Martin, Anne Pulliam Stocks, and Linda Diehl Tiano
Executive Assistant: Debra Smith

TECHNICAL
Managing Editor: Barbara Marguerite McClintock
Senior Technical Writer: Jennifer Potts Hutchings
Technical Writers: Susan McManus Johnson and Theresa Hicks Young
Copy Editor: Susan Frazier
Production Assistant: Sharon Gillam

EDITORIAL
Managing Editor: Linda L. Trimble
Senior Associate Editors: Susan McManus Johnson and Terri Leming Davidson
Associate Editors: Darla Burdette Kelsay and Stacey Robertson Marshall

ART
Book/Magazine Graphic Art Director: Diane Thomas
Graphic Artist/Illustrator: Chris Bawiec
Color Technician: Mark Hawkins
Photography Stylists: Ellen J. Clifton, Sondra Daniel, Tiffany Huffman, Elizabeth Lackey, and Janna Laughlin
Staff Photographer: Russell Ganser
Publishing Systems Administrator: Becky Riddle
Publishing Systems Assistants: Myra Means and Chris Wertenberger

PROMOTIONS
Managing Editor: Alan Caudle
Associate Editor: Steven M. Cooper
Designer: Dale Rowett
Art Director: Linda Lovette Smart

BUSINESS STAFF

Publisher: Rick Barton
Vice President and General Manager: Thomas L. Carlisle
Vice President, Finance: Tom Siebenmorgen
Vice President, Retail Marketing: Bob Humphrey
Director of Corporate Planning and Development:
Laticia Mull Cornett
Vice President, National Accounts: Pam Stebbins

Retail Marketing Director: Margaret Sweetin
General Merchandise Manager: Cathy Laird
Vice President, Operations: Jim Dittrich
Distribution Director: Rob Thieme
Retail Customer Service Manager: Wanda Price
Print Production Manager: Fred F. Pruss

Library of Congress Catalog Number 98-65089
International Standard Book Number 1-57486-172-7

10 9 8 7 6 5 4 3 2 1

TABLE OF CONTENTS

TABLE OF CONTENTS

TABLE OF CONTENTS

"CAN-DO" CRAFTS

Perfect "can-didates" for crafty conversions, cans come in a variety of shapes and sizes. Just look at the fabulous ideas on the next several pages, and you'll see an amazing assortment of distinctive designs featuring empty food containers! For instance, there's the bright-shining lighthouse lamp, a "Funny Farmer" water fountain, and lots of clever candle holders. Don't miss the burnished curtain tiebacks or the colorful napkin rings, both made from beverage cans!

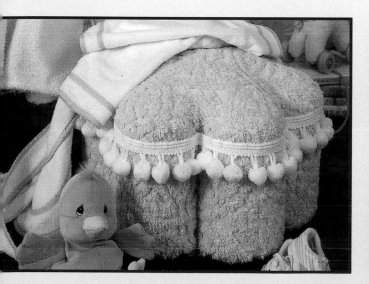

BUMBERSHOOT BIN

*W*ant to add a bit of elegance
to your entry hall? Make your own
umbrella stand! We cemented three
coffee cans together and covered
them with black vinyl to create this
fabulous bumbershoot bin. Gold
corded tassels add a special touch
of class.

UMBRELLA STAND

Recycled items: three 6" dia. x 7"h coffee
cans

You will also need plaster of paris,
household cement, duct tape, black spray
paint, clear acrylic sealer, batting, hot glue
gun, black vinyl fabric, $^1/_2$" dia. gold cord
without tassels, and $^1/_2$" dia. gold cord
with tassels.

*Allow household cement, paint, and
sealer to dry after each application.*

1. Use a can opener to remove bottoms
from two cans.
2. Follow manufacturer's instructions to
fill remaining can with plaster to a depth
of 1"; allow to harden.
3. Placing can with plaster on bottom,
stack and use household cement to glue
cans together. Wrap duct tape around
each seam to secure. Spray paint inside of

stand black. Apply two to three coats of
sealer to inside of stand.
4. Measure height of stand. Measure
around stand. Cut a piece from batting the
determined measurements. Wrap and glue
batting around stand.
5. Measure height of stand. Measure
around stand; add $^1/_2$". Cut a piece from

vinyl the determined measurements.
Overlapping ends at back, wrap and glue
vinyl around stand.
6. Trimming to fit, glue cord without
tassels around bottom of stand. Tie cord
with tassels around top of stand; spot glue
to secure.

FASHIONABLE FLOWER

It's the little things that count when it comes to home decor, and this clever drapery tieback is an accent you won't want to miss! The dimensional flower is created using layered pieces cut from aluminum cans. To give the flower an aged look, rub on a gold finish over a layer of black spray paint.

FLOWER TIEBACK ACCENT

Recycled items: four 12-oz. aluminum beverage cans for each tieback

You will also need utility scissors, white spray primer, black spray paint, gold rub-on metallic finish, paper towel, household cement, hot glue gun, and a gold tasseled tieback.

Use household cement for all gluing unless otherwise indicated. Allow primer, paint, metallic finish, and household cement to dry after each application.

1. For each can, use utility scissors to cut through opening of can; cut away and discard top.
2. For flower petals, trim three cans to within 3" from bottoms. Beginning at cut edge and cutting to outer bottom edge of

can, cut down sides of each can at 1" intervals to make petals. Flatten cans with petals extending outward. Trim each petal to a point.
3. For flower center, trim remaining can to within 1¼" from bottom. Beginning at cut edge and cutting to outer bottom edge of can, cut down sides of can at ½" intervals to make petals. Flatten can with petals extending outward. Trim corners from each petal.

4. Apply primer to each layer of flower. Spray paint each layer of flower black. Working with small sections at a time, carefully rub gold finish over layers; remove excess with paper towel.
5. Offsetting petals, layer and glue petals and flower center together.
6. Hot glue flower to tieback as desired.

LADYBUG, LADYBUG

*I*magine how much fun you'll have watching the birds discover this snug ladybug birdhouse! Created using a painted coffee can and craft foam, the fanciful house is an adorable accent for your deck.

LADYBUG BIRDHOUSE

Recycled items: 6¹/₈" dia. x 6³/₄"h coffee can with lid and a twig
You will also need a drawing compass, craft knife, cutting mat, black metal paint, paintbrush, low-temperature glue gun, 1" dia. wiggle eyes, push pin, garden clippers, hammer, nail, one 7" length and one 34" length of medium-gauge craft wire, tracing paper, and red and black craft foam.

1. Remove lid from can. Measuring 1¹/₄" from rim, use compass to draw a 1¹/₂" dia. circle on lid. Use craft knife to carefully cut out opening.

2. Paint can and lid black; allow to dry.

3. Position and glue eyes on lid. For perch, use push pin to make a pilot hole ¹/₂" below opening in lid. Use garden clippers to cut a 1¹/₂" long twig; insert in hole.

4. Use hammer and nail to punch a hole in one side of can ³/₈" from rim at top of can and ³/₈" from rim at bottom of can.

5. For hanger, thread one end of 34" length of wire through one hole; twist inside can to secure. Shape wire as desired. Thread remaining end of wire through remaining hole; twist inside can to secure. Replace lid.

6. Trace wing pattern, page 142, onto tracing paper; cut out. Draw around pattern twice on red craft foam; cut out wings. Rough cut sixteen ¹/₂" dia. to ³/₄" dia. circles for spots from black craft foam. Glue spots to wings. Glue wings to top of can.

7. For antennae, center and wrap 7" length of wire around end of hanger near top rim. Shape ends of antennae as desired.

PARTY LIGHTS

*Y*ou won't have to skimp on the essentials when you make these inexpensive torches for your next outdoor party! Just paint single-serving snack chip containers and glue them to wooden dowel rods. Tea lights provide the illumination.

PARTY TORCHES

Recycled items: single-serving snack chip containers

For each torch, you will also need white spray primer; yellow, pink, green, and dark green acrylic paint; paintbrushes; 1" dia. wooden bead; 36" of wooden dowel to fit hole in bead; tracing paper; transfer paper; craft knife; cutting mat; and a hot glue gun.

Allow primer and paint to dry after each application.

1. Apply two to three coats of primer to container. Paint container desired color. Paint rim of container, bead, and dowel in contrasting color.
2. Trace flower pattern, page 153, onto tracing paper. Spacing evenly around container, use transfer paper to transfer three flowers to container. Paint flowers and grass.

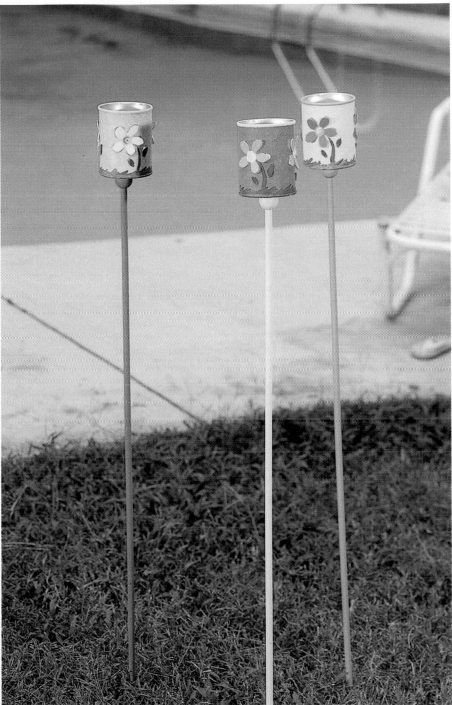

3. Use craft knife to partially cut around petals and leaves. Carefully push cut-out areas to outside.

4. Apply glue to one end of dowel. Insert dowel into bead. Center and glue bead to bottom of container.

11

*B*elieve it or not, a princess resides behind this door! Our royal sign is created from an aluminum can, and she's ready to greet all who enter your favorite little girl's room. Add a silk-petal skirt, a crown made from pull tabs, and a hairpin "scepter"; then personalize the sign with her name.

PRINCESS ROOM SIGN

Recycled items: 12-oz. aluminum beverage can, three pull tabs, and a large hairpin

You will also need utility scissors; white spray primer; gold and pink spray paint; white, peach, pink, dark pink, blue, and black acrylic paint; paintbrushes; tracing paper; transfer paper; white craft foam; low-temperature glue gun; petals from a silk flower; white craft string pearls; one 8" length each of fine-gauge and medium-gauge craft wire; household cement; assorted acrylic jewels; decorative-edge craft scissors; pink dimensional paint; pink embroidery floss; and a push pin.

Use hot glue for all gluing unless otherwise indicated. Allow primer, paint, and household cement to dry after each application.

1. Use utility scissors to cut through opening of beverage can, then cut away top; discard top. Use both hands to hold can with thumbs below bottom rim. Using thumbs, press on can to bend bottom rim down (Fig. 1). Flatten can.

Fig. 1

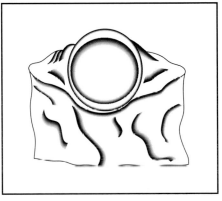

2. For body, apply primer to all sides of can. Spray paint all sides of can pink. For head, paint bottom of can peach.
3. Trace face pattern, page 135, onto tracing paper. Use transfer paper to transfer face to head. Paint face.
4. Trace patterns, page 135, onto tracing paper; cut out. Draw around patterns on craft foam; cut out shapes. Painting on both sides, paint arms pink, hands peach, and shoes black. Glue arms and legs to can.

5. For skirt, layer and glue petals around bottom of body. Wrap and glue pearls around body above petals.
6. For crown, use fine-gauge craft wire to wire three pull tabs together side by side. Spray paint crown gold. Use household cement to glue crown to top of head. Glue acrylic jewels to crown and around face as desired.
7. For scepter, glue acrylic jewels along hairpin as desired. Use household cement to glue scepter to arm, then hand to scepter.
8. For sign, use craft scissors to cut a $2^{3}/_{4}$" x $3^{3}/_{4}$" piece from craft foam. Use dimensional paint to write message on sign. Using four strands of floss, work *Running Stitches*, page 158, $^{1}/_{4}$" from edge around sign. Use household cement to glue sign to remaining arm.
9. For hanger, use push pin to carefully punch two holes 1" apart in back of character. Thread medium-gauge craft wire through holes; twist to secure.

BLAST FROM THE PAST

Our handy organizer lamp is a real blast from the past! Cover assorted cans with retro fabrics to create the trio of canisters; then trim the shade of the lamp with ribbon and bead dangles. What a groovy way to bring back memories of the good old days!

RETRO LAMP ORGANIZER

Recycled items: three assorted cans to fit on base of lamp

You will also need white spray primer, yellow acrylic paint, paintbrush, white card stock, spray adhesive, assorted fabrics, hot glue gun, 5/8"w grosgrain ribbon in assorted colors, household cement, desk lamp with flat base, clear nylon thread, 6mm crystal faceted beads, and tri-beads in assorted colors.

Use hot glue for all gluing unless otherwise indicated. Allow primer, paint, and household cement to dry after each application.

1. For each can, apply primer to inside of can. Paint inside of can yellow.
2. Measure height of can between rims. Measure around can. Cut a piece from card stock the determined measurements. Apply spray adhesive to one side of card stock. Smooth card stock around can.
3. Measure height of can; add 1/2". Measure around can; add 1/2". Cut a piece from fabric the determined measurements. Apply spray adhesive to wrong side of fabric. Overlapping fabric at back and with 1/2" of fabric extending above rim, smooth fabric around can. Clipping as necessary, fold fabric to inside of can; spot glue to secure. Trimming to fit, glue a length of ribbon around can 1/8" from top.

4. Arrange cans on base of lamp and use household cement to secure. Trimming to fit, use household cement to glue a length of ribbon around side edges of lamp base.
5. For each bead strand, cut a 5" length of thread. Thread one faceted bead onto center of thread length. Matching thread ends, fold thread length in half. Thread one tri-bead onto doubled thread. Alternating faceted beads with tri-beads,

repeat to add three faceted beads and two tri-beads to strand.
6. For beaded trim, measure around bottom of lampshade. Cut a length of ribbon the determined measurement. Spacing evenly, glue thread ends of bead strands to wrong side of ribbon. Use household cement to glue ribbon around edge of lampshade.

14

CRAFTY "CRAYON"

*N*o more hunting for your child's art supplies! We've created this colorful crayon look-alike to keep them handy. Just cover a potato chip canister with brightly colored card stock and paint a flowerpot to provide a lid. Star motifs personalize the container.

ART SUPPLY CONTAINER

Recycled item: 3" dia. x 9¹/₂"h snack chip container with lid

You will also need white spray primer; 3" dia. clay flowerpot; yellow spray paint; household cement; yellow, red, and blue card stock; craft glue; tracing paper; and a black permanent medium-point marker.

Use craft glue for all gluing unless otherwise indicated. Allow primer, paint, and glue to dry after each application.

1. Remove lid from container.
2. Apply primer to flowerpot, lid, and container. Spray paint flowerpot, lid, and container yellow.
3. Use household cement to glue rim of flowerpot to top of lid.

4. Measure height of container; subtract 1". Measure around container; add ¹/₂". Cut a piece from yellow card stock the determined measurements. Overlapping ends at back, center and glue card stock piece around container.
5. Measure around container; add ¹/₂". Cut two strips of red card stock 1¹/₄"w by the determined measurement. Cut two strips of blue card stock ¹/₂"w by the determined measurement. Overlapping ends at back, layer and glue red, then blue strips around container ¹/₄" from edges of yellow card stock piece.
6. Trace star pattern, page 145, onto tracing paper; cut out. Draw around pattern desired number of times on red and blue card stock; cut out shapes. Use marker to write "My Stuff" on one star. Arrange and glue stars on container.
7. Replace lid on container.

PUPPET SURPRISE

POP-UP PUPPET

Kids love to be surprised, and this perky pop-up puppet is sure to provide hours of giggles. At first glance, it seems to be just a decorated container — but look again! It's a funny-face friend! Bright fabric covers the can and creates a collar for the clown. Finish with jumbo rickrack and pom-poms.

Recycled items: 4" dia. x 5½"h coffee can with lid and a plastic bottle cap

You will also need batting; craft glue; fabric; drawing compass; rickrack; three 12mm pom-poms for "buttons"; tracing paper; white, red, and black craft foam; one 9mm pom-pom for nose; 2½" dia. plastic foam ball for head, black permanent fine-point marker; yarn; craft knife; cutting mat; bias tape to coordinate with fabric; acrylic paint to coordinate with fabric; paintbrush; and 5" of 5/16" dia. wooden dowel.

Allow glue and paint to dry after each application.

1. Remove lid from can; set aside. Use a can opener to remove bottom from can.
2. Measure height of can between rims. Measure around can. Cut a piece from batting the determined measurements. Glue batting around can.
3. Measure height of can between rims; add 1". Measure around can; add ½". Cut a piece from fabric the determined measurements. Overlapping fabric at back, glue fabric around can. Pleating as necessary, glue excess fabric to inside top and bottom of can.

4. For pop-up body piece, use compass to draw a 12" dia. circle on wrong side of fabric; cut out. Use compass to draw a 4" dia. circle in center of pop-up body piece; cut out. Gathering to fit, glue outer edge of pop-up body piece along top edge of outside of can. Trimming to fit and covering raw edges, glue rickrack along top edge of can. Glue "buttons" to can.
5. Trace eye and mouth patterns, page 135, onto tracing paper; cut out. Draw around upper eye on black craft foam, lower eye on white craft foam, and mouth on red craft foam; cut out shapes. Arrange and glue eyes, mouth, and nose to head. Use marker to add pupils to eyes.
6. For hair, cut several 4" lengths from yarn. Fold each length in half. Glue folds of yarn around head.
7. For hat, use compass to draw a 3¼" dia. circle at center of coffee can lid; use craft knife to cut out circle. Use compass to draw a 3¼" dia. circle on wrong side of fabric; cut out. Glue fabric to lid piece. Trimming to fit and inserting edges of hat into fold of bias tape, glue bias tape around edge of hat. Paint plastic bottle cap; allow to dry. Center and glue bottle cap to hat. Glue hat to head.
8. For collar, use compass to draw a 4" dia. circle on wrong side of fabric; cut out. Cut a small hole at center of collar. Trimming to fit, glue rickrack along outside edge of collar.
9. Apply glue to one end of dowel; insert 1½" into bottom of head. Place dowel through small hole at center of collar; glue to bottom of head to secure. Place dowel through hole in center of pop-up body piece; gather and glue pop-up body piece around dowel under collar.

Wherever your "port of call" may be, you'll never get lost with this lamp to light your way! Created with cardboard canisters and a can, our detailed lighthouse will breathe life into any room. A lamp kit hidden inside makes the nautical accent light up.

LIGHTHOUSE LAMP

Recycled items: 5" dia. x 5³/₄"h cardboard container with lid, 3" dia. x 2"h can, 5" dia. x 8¹/₄"h cardboard container, and a ³/₄" x 7" x 7" box lid for base

You will also need hammer; awl; household cement; 8" square of foam core board; drawing compass; craft knife; cutting mat; four toothpicks; craft saw; 2¹/₂"h flat wooden clothespins; white spray primer; masking tape; white, red, and black acrylic paint; paintbrushes; clear acrylic spray sealer; glossy wood-tone spray; craft drill; hot glue gun; two 22" lengths of kite string; needle with eye large enough to accommodate string; hacksaw; ³/₈" dia. threaded I.P. pipe stem; 40" length of floral wire; lamp kit; and a lampshade.

Use household cement for all gluing unless otherwise indicated. Allow household cement, primer, paint, sealer, and wood-tone spray to dry after each application.

1. Remove lid from 5" dia. x 5³/₄"h cardboard container; set aside. For beacon, use hammer and awl to punch a ³/₈" dia. hole in center of closed end of container and in center of closed end of can.
2. For lighthouse, glue open end of 5" dia. x 5³/₄"h cardboard container to open end of 5" dia. x 8¹/₄"h cardboard container. Aligning holes, glue open end of beacon to top of lighthouse.
3. For catwalk, draw around lid from 5" dia. x 5³/₄"h cardboard container on foam core board. Use compass to draw a second circle 1" outside first circle. Use craft knife to cut out catwalk along drawn lines.
4. For rails, use saw to cut "legs" from clothespins.
5. Apply primer to lighthouse, beacon, catwalk, rails, and base.
6. Beginning 2¹/₈" from bottom of lighthouse, use masking tape to mask off three evenly spaced 1⁷/₈"w stripes around lighthouse. Paint lighthouse red. Remove tape. Mask painted areas. Paint lighthouse white. Remove masking tape. Paint a 2" x 3¹/₈" black door on front of lighthouse. Spacing evenly around beacon, use masking tape to mask off ⁷/₈" x 1⁷/₈" "windows." Paint beacon black. Remove masking tape. Mask painted areas. Paint windows white. Remove masking tape. Paint catwalk and rails white. Paint base black.
7. Apply one coat of sealer to lighthouse, beacon, catwalk, rails, and base. Lightly apply wood-tone, then a second coat of sealer to lighthouse, beacon, catwalk, and rails.

8. Place catwalk on lighthouse just below top. Use a pencil to lightly draw four evenly spaced lines across catwalk from outside edge to inside edge of catwalk. Mark a dot on lighthouse where each line ends. Remove catwalk. Use hammer and awl to punch holes in sides of lighthouse at dots. With ends extending slightly beyond outside of catwalk, insert one toothpick horizontally through catwalk at each drawn line. Aligning drawn lines on catwalk and dots on lighthouse, replace catwalk on lighthouse; spot glue to secure. Erase drawn lines. Push toothpicks through catwalk and into lighthouse until ends are flush with outside edge of catwalk.
9. Drill two holes ¹/₂" apart through flat side of each rail (Fig. 1). Spacing evenly, hot glue rails onto catwalk. Use needle to thread one length of string through top holes and one length of string through bottom holes; knot at back of lighthouse to secure.

Fig. 1

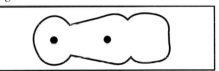

10. Measure height of lighthouse; add ¹/₂". Use hacksaw to cut a length from pipe stem the determined measurement.
11. Use craft knife to cut a ¹/₂" square in bottom back of lighthouse. Thread wire down through holes in center of beacon and lighthouse, then out hole in back of lighthouse. Wrap end of wire in back of lighthouse around lamp cord. To thread lamp cord, carefully pull wire up through center of lighthouse, then through pipe stem. Thread pipe stem down through holes in center of lighthouse. Follow manufacturer's instructions to assemble lamp.
12. Glue lighthouse to base. Place lampshade on lamp.

CANISTER CRITTERS

*D*oes the clutter of half-empty packages in your cabinets really "bug" you? Get organized with these cute canisters! Simply cover discarded cardboard containers with torn pieces of fabric; then finish with strips of fabric and buttons. Fashion the critter tops by attaching wing cutouts to painted plastic lids.

BUG-TOP CANISTERS

Recycled items: two cardboard canisters with lids and two additional 3" dia. plastic lids from cardboard canisters

You will also need assorted fabrics; spray adhesive; craft glue; pinking shears; hot glue gun; assorted black buttons; yellow, red, and black acrylic paint; paintbrushes; tracing paper; wire cutters; medium-gauge craft wire; and pliers.

Allow paint to dry after each application.

BUMBLEBEE CANISTER
1. Measure height of one canister between rims. Measure around canister; add ¹/₂". Tear a piece from fabric the determined measurements. Apply spray adhesive to outside of canister. Overlapping ends at

back, smooth fabric around canister. Use craft glue to secure overlapped edge; allow to dry.
2. Measure around canister; add ¹/₂". Use pinking shears to cut a 1¹/₄"w strip from fabric the determined measurement. Apply spray adhesive to wrong side of fabric strip. Overlapping ends at back, smooth fabric strip around canister.
3. Hot glue buttons to canister as desired.
4. Paint canister lid yellow. Paint black stripes on lid.
5. Trace wings pattern, page 145, onto tracing paper; cut out. Placing outer edge of pattern along rim of one 3" dia. lid, draw around pattern on lid; cut out wings. Arrange and glue wings on lid of canister.
6. Use wire cutters to cut two 3" lengths of craft wire for antennae. Use pliers to

shape ¹/₂" of one end of each antenna into a spiral. Glue antennae to back of button. Position and glue button to rim of lid for head.

LADYBUG CANISTER
1. Follow Steps 1 - 3 of Bumblebee Canister.
2. Paint canister lid black.
3. Trace wings pattern, page 145, onto tracing paper; cut out. Placing outer edge of pattern along rim of remaining 3" dia. lid, draw around pattern on lid; cut out wings. Paint wings red. Paint black dots on wings. Arrange and glue wings to lid of canister.
4. Follow Step 6 of Bumblebee Canister to complete canister.

TERRIFIC GIFT TOTES

Whatever the occasion, you'll have the perfect offering when you craft these nifty can containers! Wrap painted cans with fabric and fashion their handles from craft wire; then write your own message or greeting on hand-colored labels. Now you're ready to fill your totes with gifts for special friends!

GIFT HOLDERS

Recycled items: assorted cans
You will also need white spray primer; yellow, red, or blue spray paint; fabrics; hot glue gun; colored pencils; photocopy of label (page 152); black permanent medium-point marker; spray adhesive; hammer; nail; wire cutters; and medium-gauge craft wire.

Allow primer and paint to dry after each application.

1. For each gift holder, apply primer to inside and outside of one can. Spray paint inside and outside of can desired color.
2. Measure around can; add ¹/₂". Measure height of can between rims; subtract ¹/₂". Tear a piece from fabric the determined measurements. Overlapping at back, center and glue fabric around can.
3. Use colored pencils to color label; cut out. Use marker to write message on label. Apply spray adhesive to wrong side of label. Center and smooth label onto can.
4. Use hammer and nail to punch a hole in each side of can. Use wire cutters to cut an 18" length of wire. For handle, insert one end of wire through one hole; bend up and twist to secure. Shape loops in wire as desired. Insert opposite end of wire through hole in opposite side of can; bend up and twist to secure.

FUNKY CHICKEN

*K*now someone who's feeling a little blue? Our bobbly-wobbly bird is sure to bring smiles to folks of all ages as he sways in the gentlest breeze! Made with cans, this funny speckled rooster has legs made from the spiral bindings of notebooks and a perch fashioned of driftwood. What a whimsical way to recycle!

LOONY BIRD

Recycled items: three aluminum beverage cans, one 2¹/₂" long piece and two 5" long pieces of spiral binding, 3³/₈"h x 2" dia. can for body, and a piece of driftwood at least 1" x 6" x 10"

You will also need utility scissors; tracing paper; black permanent medium-point marker; one 5" length and one 16" length of 16-gauge craft wire; grey spray primer; white, yellow, orange, red, and black acrylic paint; paintbrushes; household cement; hammer; nail; craft drill; and a hot glue gun.

Allow primer, paint, and household cement to dry after each application. Use household cement for all gluing unless otherwise indicated.

1. Remove pull tab from each beverage can; discard. Use utility scissors to cut through opening and down to bottom of each can. Cut top and bottom from each can. Flatten side can pieces. Cut opening tab from inside top of each can (Fig. 1); discard remainder of can tops. Cutting in the groove around can bottoms, cut circles from bottoms of two cans for head pieces; discard remaining can bottoms.

Fig. 1

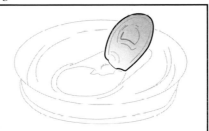

2. Trace patterns, page 155, onto tracing paper; cut out. Use marker to draw once around comb, twice around foot and wing, and three times around feather patterns on flattened can pieces. Use utility scissors to cut out shapes.

3. Apply primer to all sides of tabs, head, comb, feet, feathers, spiral binding pieces, craft wire pieces, and body. Paint all sides of one opening tab (wattle) and comb orange. Paint feet, 5" long spiral binding pieces (legs), 16" craft wire length, and one side of each remaining opening tab (beak) yellow. Paint head pieces, 2¹/₂" long spiral binding piece (neck), 5" craft wire length, body, wings, feathers, and opposite side of each beak piece red. Paint yellow dots on comb and wattle. Paint one eye on each head piece. Paint white dots on head pieces.

4. For head, inserting comb and wattle between circles, glue cut edges of head pieces together. For beak, with yellow facing out, bend each beak piece in half. With curved edge of one beak piece overlapping remaining beak piece, glue beak pieces together. Glue beak to head.

5. Measuring from rim of closed end of can for body, use hammer and nail to punch one hole ¹/₈" from rim to insert neck and two holes ¹/₂" apart and 1" from rim, across from hole for neck, to insert legs.

6. Working from inside body, insert one end of red wire through hole for neck. Glue one end of neck close to hole. Wrap wire over end of neck and thread back down through hole; twist inside body to secure. Glue head to opposite end of neck.

7. Bend ¹/₂" of blunt end of each feather at a 90° angle to form flap. Glue flap of each feather and wings to body. Paint white dots on body, wings, and feathers.

8. Use craft drill to drill two holes 1¹/₂" apart in center of driftwood.

9. To assemble bird, insert one end of yellow wire up through drilled hole in driftwood. Thread one leg onto wire. Working from outside, thread wire through one leg hole in body, then down through second leg hole. Thread remaining leg onto wire. Insert wire end through remaining drilled hole in driftwood. Hot glue wire ends to bottom of driftwood to secure.

10. Glue feet to driftwood at bottom of legs.

CATCH-ALL CANS

*H*ere's a fabulous way to organize those cluttersome odds and ends while adding a touch of country cheer to your home! Covered in gingham gift wrap and decorated with veggie-motif cutouts, ordinary food cans become handy little pails.

HANGING CATCH-ALL CANS

Recycled items: four 4" dia. x 5³/₈"h cans and greeting cards
You will also need red and tan acrylic paint, paintbrushes, wooden peg hanger with four pegs, wrapping paper, spray adhesive, craft glue, rubber bands, hammer, nail, wire cutters, and medium-gauge craft wire.

Allow paint and glue to dry after each application.

1. Paint peg hanger tan. Mix one part red paint with one part water. Use mixture to paint a ¹/₄"w border around pegs. Using unthinned red paint, paint red squares along border.
2. For each can, measure height of can between rims. Measure around can; add ¹/₂". Cut a piece from wrapping paper the determined measurements. Apply spray adhesive to wrong side of wrapping paper piece. Overlapping ends at back, position and smooth wrapping paper piece around can.
3. Cut desired motifs from cards. Use craft glue to glue one motif to front of each can; allow to dry.

4. Use hammer and nail to punch a hole in opposite sides of can ¹/₂" from rim.
5. For each handle, use wire cutters to cut an 18" length of craft wire. Working from the inside, thread 3" of one end of wire through one hole on one side of can; bend wire up and twist to secure. If desired, curl end of wire around a pencil; remove pencil. Repeat to thread remaining end of wire through hole in opposite side of can.
6. Hang cans on peg hanger.

SPRING RINGS

Accent your springtime table with pretty napkin rings that began as aluminum cans. After cutting and shaping your flowers, paint them in fresh colors and glue sheer ribbon to the backs. Now you can tie up your napkins with flair!

NAPKIN RINGS

Recycled items: one 12-oz. aluminum beverage can for each napkin ring
You will also need utility scissors, white spray primer, desired colors of acrylic paint, paintbrushes, hot glue gun, and 20" of 1 1/2"w sheer ribbon.

Allow primer and paint to dry after each application.

1. For each napkin ring, use utility scissors to cut through opening of one beverage can; cut away and discard top. Trim can to within 1/2" of bottom of can. For flower, beginning at cut edge and cutting to outer bottom edge of can, cut down sides of can at 1/2" intervals to make petals. Flatten can with petals extending outward.

2. Apply primer to flower. Paint flower as desired.

3. Center and glue ribbon to back of flower. Notch ribbon ends.

FUNNY FARMER

*A*dd a bit of whimsy to your garden or patio with our irresistible fountain. Made from assorted-size cans, this funny farmer actually sprays water through a "garden hose." Surround his feet with silk vegetables so everyone can see how his garden grows!

CAN MAN FOUNTAIN

Recycled items: 12-oz. aluminum beverage can, 6" dia. x 4^1/$_2$"h can for body, 3^1/$_4$" dia. x 4^1/$_4$"h can for head, two 2^7/$_8$" dia. x 4^1/$_4$"h cans for legs, two 2^1/$_2$" dia. x 4"h cans for arms, 2^5/$_8$" x 3^3/$_4$" can with rounded corners for support, 11" dia. tin, foam produce container, plastic mesh produce container, and two pull tabs

You will also need utility scissors; white spray primer; 1¼"w masking tape; white, cream, peach, pink, red, light blue, blue, brown, and black metal paint; paintbrushes; household sponges; tracing paper; transfer paper; black permanent medium-point marker; ³/₈" dia. wooden dowel; ½" dia. clear rubber tubing; green spray paint; hammer; nail; craft drill; ½"l bolts with nuts; household cement; green and tan card stock; decorative-edge craft scissors; craft glue; corrugated craft cardboard; brown plastic canvas; foam brush; silicone adhesive; pump for a large fountain; jumbo craft stick; 8" dia. straw hat including brim; 1½" x 16" piece of bandanna print fabric; and artificial vegetables and greenery.

Refer to Painting Techniques, page 156, before beginning project. Allow primer, paint, household cement, craft glue, and silicone adhesive to dry after each application. Use household cement for all gluing unless otherwise indicated.

1. Use utility scissors to cut through opening and down to bottom of beverage can; cut away and discard top and bottom. Flatten can piece.

2. Apply primer to both sides of flattened beverage can piece, all cans, and outside of tin.

3. Cut a 15¼" length of masking tape. Wrap tape around closed end of body. Cut a 2" length of masking tape; center tape between ends of first tape piece.

4. Paint head and both sides of flattened beverage can piece peach. Paint legs and body light blue. Lightly sponge paint legs and body blue. Remove tape. Mask around unpainted areas of body. Paint arms and unpainted areas on body red. Remove tape.

5. Trace face pattern, page 140, onto tracing paper. With closed end at top, use transfer paper to transfer face to head. Paint face. Using short brush strokes and brown paint, paint hair.

6. For base, paint tin cream. Cut a 1" square from sponge. Sponge paint red squares evenly around rim of tin. Use marker to outline squares with wavy lines and to add dots between squares.

7. Insert dowel into tubing. Spray paint tubing green. Remove dowel.

8. Using hammer and nail, punch one hole in each arm at open end 1¼" from rim. Punch one hole in each side of body at closed end 1¼" from rim. Punch a hole in closed end of right arm; use craft drill to enlarge hole to ½". Aligning holes, use bolts and nuts to attach arms to body. Center and glue head on closed end of body. Center and glue one end of support inside closed end of body. Glue legs to remaining end of support.

9. Trace hands and ears patterns, page 140, onto tracing paper; cut out. Use marker to draw around patterns on flattened can piece; cut out shapes. Fold hands and ears as indicated by dotted line on pattern. Use marker to draw details on ears. Glue ears to head and hands to arms.

10. For sign, trace message pattern, page 140, onto tracing paper. Use transfer paper to transfer words to tan card stock. Use marker to draw over words. Use craft scissors to cut out sign ⅛" from words. Use marker to add details to sign. Center and use craft glue to glue sign on green card stock. Leaving a ⅛" green border,

cut out sign. Center and use craft glue to glue sign on corrugated cardboard. Leaving a ¼" cardboard border at top and bottom and ½" cardboard border at sides, use craft scissors to cut out sign. Use craft glue to glue sign to base.

11. Use marker to draw around base on canvas; cut out circle ¼" inside drawn line. Cut a wedge-shaped opening from edge of circle large enough to accommodate tubing, pump cord, and foam produce container.

12. Use foam brush to apply silicone adhesive to inside of tin.

13. To assemble fountain, with base front forward, place pump in back of base on right side. Place foam produce container upside down in back of base beside pump. Place mesh produce container upside down in front of foam produce container. Attach one end of tubing to pump. With tubing and pump cord extending through opening, place canvas piece over pump and produce containers. Insert craft stick in foam produce container. With craft stick inside one leg, place can man on foam produce container. Thread tubing around back of can man and through hole in closed end of arm.

14. Glue hat to head and pull tabs to body. Knot fabric piece around neck. Arrange vegetables and greenery in base.

15. Follow pump manufacturer's recommendations to fill base with water.

KITCHEN GARDEN

*I*magine having fresh herbs from your own indoor garden . . . no matter what the season! Made from three instant beverage mix cans and wrapped in raffia ribbon for natural appeal, this little planter will add rustic charm to your windowsill.

HERB PLANTER

Recycled items: three 2¹⁄₈" x 2¹⁄₂" x 4" cans with rounded corners

You will also need yellow, green, and tan acrylic paint; paintbrushes; crackle medium; hot glue gun; 2"w burlap ribbon; natural and green raffia; natural card stock; decorative-edge craft scissors; corrugated craft cardboard; black permanent medium-point marker; craft sticks; and craft picks.

Allow paint and crackle medium to dry after each application.

1. Paint outside of each can green. Follow manufacturer's instructions to apply crackle medium to outside of each can. Paint outside of each can tan.
2. For planter, glue cans together side by side.
3. Measure around planter. Cut a length of burlap ribbon the determined measurement. Fold ribbon length in half lengthwise. Center and glue ribbon length around planter. Measure around planter; add 5". Cut several lengths from each color of raffia the determined measurement. Knot raffia lengths together around planter.
4. For each herb label, cut one 1" x 2" piece from card stock. Use marker to write desired herb name and add details to card stock piece. Use craft scissors to cut one 1¹⁄₂" x 2¹⁄₂" piece from corrugated cardboard. Center and glue label to corrugated cardboard piece.
5. For each plant poke, paint one craft stick yellow. Glue one craft pick to one end of craft stick. Glue label to opposite end of craft stick.

"CHEEP" BIRD FEEDER

*Y*ou don't have to buy a costly bird feeder to nourish nature's little warblers. Construct one from an empty coffee can painted with a cheery design! Side panels, cut from the plastic lid and glued to each end, keep the birdseed inside, and a wooden dowel offers the birds a place to perch.

BIRD FEEDER

Recycled item: 4" dia. x 5½"h coffee can with lid

You will also need white spray primer; white, yellow, red, blue, green, dark green, and black metal paint; household sponges; paintbrushes; 8½" of ¼" dia. wooden dowel; craft knife; cutting mat; household cement; and 24" of jute twine.

Refer to Painting Techniques, page 156, before beginning project. Allow primer, paint, and household cement to dry after each application.

1. Remove lid from can; set aside. Use a can opener to remove bottom from can. Turn can on its side.

2. Apply primer to outside of can. Sponge paint half of can blue for sky, then remaining half of can dark green for grass. Sponge paint white clouds on sky. Paint blackbirds on sky. Lightly sponge paint grass green. Paint ladybugs and flowers on grass as desired. Paint dowel dark green.

3. Including rim, use craft knife to cut lid in half. Measuring from straight edge, trim 1" from each half of lid. Glue curved edges to openings of can at each end.

4. Extending 3" beyond each end of can, glue dowel to bottom of can for perch. For hanger, knot ends of twine together inside can. Glue twine to inside top of can at each end to secure.

CANDLE CACHET

*R*escue those cans and jars from the trash and use them to create these lovely candle holders. Each holder features ribbon trims, buttons, and flower accents that you can glue on in a jiffy. You'll have elegant containers to fill with your favorite scented candles in no time!

CREATIVE CANDLE HOLDERS

Recycled items: three assorted cans and two baby food jars

You will also need grey spray primer, silver spray paint, hot glue gun, assorted ribbons and decorative trims, and items to decorate holders (we used artificial flowers and buttons).

Allow primer and paint to dry after each application.

1. Apply primer to each can. Spray paint each can.
2. Trimming to fit, tie or glue ribbons and trims around cans and jars. Glue decorative items to cans and jars as desired.

LOVELY LUMINARIAS

*N*o *outdoor party would be complete without these pretty hanging luminarias! Simply punch designs into the cans using a hammer and a nail; then thread beads onto the hangers to add sparkling color.*

HANGING CAN CANDLE HOLDERS

Recycled items: cans
You will also need tracing paper, tape, towel, heavy-duty gloves, hammer, nail, wire cutters, medium-gauge craft wire, and assorted beads.

1. For each holder, fill one can to rim with water; freeze until water is frozen solid.
2. Trace desired pattern, page 151, onto tracing paper; cut out.
3. Arrange pattern on can; use tape to secure.
4. Place can pattern side up on towel. Wearing gloves use hammer and nail to punch a hole at each dot on pattern. (Refreeze can if necessary to keep water frozen.)
5. Repeat Steps 3 and 4, moving patterns for desired placement of design. Spacing evenly, use hammer and nail to punch three holes 1/4" from rim of can.
6. Run warm water into can to melt ice; dry can completely.
7. Use wire cutters to cut three 14" lengths of craft wire. Working from the inside, thread 4" of one end of each wire length through one hole at rim; bend up and twist to secure. If desired, curl end of wire around a pencil; remove pencil. Thread beads onto wires as desired. Twist remaining ends of wires together. Bend wires into a hook.

COOKIE CAPERS

*B*efore they make another cookie raid, let your brownie burglars know you're onto their felonious ways with a quote from a popular children's game. This tasteful treat keeper starts with a large can and finishes with a cookie cutter handle!

COOKIE CAN

Recycled items: 6¹/₈" dia. x 6⁵/₈"h can with lid, star-shaped metal cookie cutter, and a large brown paper bag

You will also need white spray primer, yellow and blue spray paint, fabric, spray adhesive, 4¹/₄" x 21¹/₂" piece of poster board, hot glue gun, ³/₄" x 3¹/₂" hook and loop fastener, tracing paper, transfer paper, black permanent medium-point marker, drawing compass, batting, ¹/₄"w ribbon, and heavy-duty thread.

Allow primer and paint to dry after each application.

1. Remove lid from can. Turn can upside down. Apply primer to outside of can and cookie cutter. Spray paint outside of can yellow and cookie cutter blue.
2. For cover, cut a 7" x 21¹/₂" piece from fabric. Apply spray adhesive to wrong side

of fabric piece. Overlapping to back as necessary, smooth fabric onto poster board. Glue hook side of fastener to right side of cover 1¹/₄" from one end. Glue loop side of fastener to wrong side of cover ¹/₄" from opposite end.
3. For label, cut a 2" x 9³/₈" piece from bag. Trace pattern, page 153, onto tracing paper. Use transfer paper to center and transfer words to bag piece. Use marker to draw over words and add details to label.
4. Apply spray adhesive to wrong side of label. Center and smooth label onto cover. Wrap cover around can with hook and loop fasteners joining at back.
5. For lid, use compass to draw one

8¹/₂" dia. circle on wrong side of fabric and two 6" dia. circles on batting; cut out circles. Layer and glue batting circles to lid. Overlapping onto rim of lid and pleating as necessary, glue fabric to lid. Trim fabric even with rim of lid. Trimming to fit, glue a length of ribbon around rim of lid.
6. Place cookie cutter at center of lid. To attach cookie cutter, thread needle with heavy-duty thread. Working from wrong side of lid and pulling taut, insert needle through center of lid, then over cookie cutter handle and back through lid. Repeat until cookie cutter is secure. Tie a 10" length of ribbon into a bow around cookie cutter handle. Replace lid on can.

NURSERY RHYME TUFFET

This tot-size tuffet brings to mind a favorite nursery rhyme! Chenille fabric and pom-pom fringe accent the stool, which is constructed using juice cans, cardboard, and batting. What a cute, inexpensive addition to a little one's decor!

JUICE CAN TUFFET

Recycled items: seven 4¹/₂" dia. x 8"h cans (we used 46-oz. juice cans)

You will also need batting, hot glue gun, chenille fabric, heavy-duty thread, 10" dia. cardboard circle, spray adhesive, kraft paper, and ball fringe.

1. Set aside one can for center of tuffet.
2. For each remaining can, measure height of can between rims. Measure around can. Cut a piece from batting the determined measurements. Wrap and glue batting around can.
3. Measure height of can between rims; add 4". Measure around can. Cut a piece from fabric the determined measurements. Use heavy-duty thread to baste along each long edge of fabric piece; do not trim ends. With fabric extending 2" beyond top and bottom of can, wrap and glue fabric piece around can. Pull thread ends to tightly gather fabric at top and bottom of can. Knot thread ends to secure; trim ends.
4. Arrange and glue fabric-covered cans around center can.
5. Cut a piece from fabric 1" larger than cardboard circle. Apply spray adhesive to wrong side of fabric. Clipping as necessary, smooth fabric onto cardboard. Center and glue fabric-covered cardboard onto cans for bottom of tuffet.
6. For pattern, draw around tuffet on kraft paper; cut out. Using pattern, cut enough pieces from batting to achieve desired thickness on top of tuffet. Layer and glue batting pieces on top of tuffet. Cut one piece from fabric 1" larger on all sides than pattern. Place fabric piece on top of tuffet. Make a 1" clip in fabric between each can. Using a double strand of heavy-duty thread and turning edge of fabric to wrong side to fit along top edges, blindstitch fabric around top edges of tuffet.
7. Trimming to fit, glue a length of fringe around tuffet.

Everyone loves the beach, and now you can enjoy a bit of it every day with these refreshing bathroom accessories. Cover ordinary cans and a beverage bottle with corrugated craft paper to begin; then add jute twine wrappings and shells for a seaside look.

SEASHELL BATH ENSEMBLE

Recycled items: one short and one tall can (we used 3" dia. x 1⁵/₈"h and 2⁵/₈" dia. x 3"h cans) and a glass beverage bottle

You will also need brown corrugated craft paper, craft glue, jute twine, household cement, seashells, dried leaves, coral pieces, decorative-edge craft scissors, and a craft drill.

Use craft glue for all gluing unless otherwise indicated. Allow glue to dry after each application.

1. For short can, measure around can; add ¹/₂". Cut a strip of paper 1"w by the determined measurement. Overlapping ends at back and with strip extending ¹/₂" above rim, glue paper strip around can. Fold strip to inside of can; glue to secure. Beginning and ending at back and gluing as necessary to secure, wrap jute around bottom of can to measure 1¹/₄" wide. Arrange seashells and leaves on can; use household cement to secure.

2. For tall can, measure around can; add ¹/₂". Cut a strip of paper 1⁵/₈"w by the determined measurement. Overlapping ends at back, center and glue paper strip around can. Beginning and ending at back and gluing as necessary to secure, wrap jute around top and bottom of can to measure ⁵/₈" wide. Arrange seashells, coral piece, and leaves on can; use household cement to secure.

3. For bottle, measure around bottle at widest point; add ¹/₂". Cut two strips of paper ¹/₂"w by the determined measurement. Use craft scissors to trim one edge of each strip. With 2" between strips, decorative edges facing center, and overlapping ends at back, glue strips around bottle. Beginning and ending at back and gluing as necessary to secure, wrap jute around top and bottom of bottle from outer edges of each paper strip. Tie a 16" length of jute around neck of bottle. Use household cement to glue one seashell and leaves to knot. Drill small holes in six seashells or coral pieces. For each jute streamer, thread one seashell or coral piece onto streamer; tie a knot in streamer to secure. Repeat to thread two more seashells or coral pieces onto streamer. If desired, place one shell in bottle for stopper.

BROWN BAGGIN' IT

Plain brown bags — what could be more common or overlooked? Well, take a look at them now! We'll show you how to transform ordinary bags into extraordinary decor. For instance, take a walk on the wild side with an animal print lampshade, complete with safari beads. Or check out the quick-to-make "quilt-block" wall hanging. It's a fabulous fake with very little sewing involved. From glowing luminarias to sparkling jewelry, you'll see how that stash of sacks is a gold mine of crafting resources!

"ANTIQUE" ALBUM

*I*magine their surprise when friends discover that this "antique" photo album was made using brown paper bags! Simply tear pieces from a paper bag and glue them to an album; then brush on coats of stain for an aged look. Add a brass frame and corners to complete the cover with class.

PHOTO ALBUM

Recycled items: large brown paper bags
You will also need foam brushes, craft glue, 6¼" x 6¾" photo album, antiquing stain, matte acrylic sealer, black permanent medium-point marker, ¾" x 2¾" piece of natural card stock, 1½" x 3½" rectangular brass frame charm, hot glue gun, 2" gold tassel, and four ⅜" brass corners.

1. To prepare each bag, cut bag open along one fold; cut away and discard bottom. Press bag with a warm, dry iron.
2. Carefully tear enough 1" to 2" pieces from bags to cover album. Use foam brush to apply craft glue to wrong sides of paper bag pieces. Overlapping as necessary to cover outside of album, smooth paper bag pieces onto album; allow to dry.
3. To line inside of album, cut two pieces from bag ½" smaller on all sides than front of album. Use foam brush to apply craft glue to back of paper bag pieces. Smooth pieces on inside front and back of album; allow to dry.
4. Follow *Antiquing*, page 157, to apply stain to inside and outside of album. Allowing to dry between each application, use foam brush to apply two to three

coats of sealer to inside and outside of album; allow to dry.
5. Use marker to write "Photos" on card stock piece. Insert card stock in frame.

Hot glue frame to front of album. Hot glue tassel inside opening edge of front of album and brass corners to corners of album.

SAFARI SHADE

*B*ring the distinctive look of an African safari to your decor with this eye-catching lamp! Animal bead dangles and painted spots give the paper-covered lampshade its own unique finish.

SAFARI LAMPSHADE

Recycled items: large brown paper bags
You will also need beige and brown acrylic paint, paintbrushes, lampshade, foam brush, decoupage glue, awl, waxed linen thread, wooden animal-shaped beads, and assorted wooden and metal beads.

Refer to Painting Techniques, page 156, before beginning project. Allow paint to dry after each application.

1. To prepare each bag, cut bag open along one fold; cut away and discard bottom. Press bag with a warm, dry iron.
2. Paint a beige base coat on each bag. Paint brown spots randomly over base coat.
3. Carefully tear enough 1" to 2" pieces from bags to cover lampshade. Use foam brush to apply glue to wrong sides of bag pieces. Overlapping as necessary to cover lampshade, smooth bag pieces onto lampshade; allow to dry. Allowing to dry between each application, use foam brush to apply two to three coats of glue over lampshade.
4. Use awl to punch holes at 1" intervals ¼" from bottom edge of lampshade. For each hole, cut a 10" length of thread; knot one end. String beads onto thread as desired. Working from outside, work remaining end of thread through hole in lampshade; knot end around thread at bottom of lampshade to secure. Trim thread ends.

DAZZLING DRAGONFLIES

*P*lain *brown bags make eye-catching luminarias when you add punched designs like our dazzling dragonflies painted in bright colors. Weighted with sand and lit with tea light candles, the bags are great for adding a soft glow to your garden party or lighting up a walkway.*

PAPER BAG LUMINARIAS

Recycled items: brown lunch-size paper bags

You will also need tracing paper; transfer paper; 5¹/₂" x 9" piece of heavyweight cardboard; hammer; awl; yellow, purple, and green acrylic paint; paintbrushes; black permanent fine-point marker; sand; and tea light candles.

1. For each luminaria, refold one bag and flatten. Press with a warm dry iron if necessary.
2. Trace pattern, page 143, onto tracing paper. Use transfer paper to transfer pattern onto side of paper bag without seam.
3. Insert cardboard piece inside bag. Punching through dots on pattern, use hammer and awl to punch holes in bag.
4. Allowing to dry after each application and using holes as a guide, paint dragonfly green with yellow stripes and purple wings. Use marker to add eyes and outline each hole with small dots. Remove cardboard piece.
5. Open bag. Fold top of bag ¹/₄", then 1" to outside. Fill bottom of bag with sand. Place tea light in sand.

EVENING GLAMOUR

*N*o *one will ever guess that these glamorous accessories started out as a brown paper bag! Use our geometric patterns to arrange the beads, or create your own "signature" designs. What a perfect way to dress up your favorite evening wear!*

BEADED PAPER BAG JEWELRY

Recycled item: large brown paper bag

You will also need a rolling pin, craft glue, heavy books, tracing paper, transfer paper, white paper, black dimensional paint, household cement, acrylic jewel, toothpicks, straight pins, seed beads in assorted colors, craft knife, cutting mat, black acrylic paint, paintbrush, clear acrylic spray sealer, pin back, and earring backs.

Use household cement for all gluing unless otherwise indicated.

1. To prepare bag, cut bag open along one fold; cut away and discard bottom. Press bag with a warm, dry iron.
2. Cut bag into $3^{1}/_{2}$" x 5" strips. Using rolling pin to flatten strips after each layer, layer and use craft glue to glue strips together until a $^{1}/_{8}$" thickness is

achieved. Place strips under books to keep flat; allow to dry.
3. Trace pin and earring patterns, page 148, onto tracing paper. Use transfer paper to transfer one pin and two earring patterns to white paper; cut out. Use craft glue to glue patterns to paper bag strips; allow to dry. Outline patterns with dimensional paint; allow to dry.
4. For pin, glue acrylic jewel at center of pin. Use toothpick to apply glue to outlined area at center of pin. Use straight pin to place beads in area; allow to dry.

Repeat for remaining outlined areas.
5. For each earring, use toothpick to apply glue to one outlined area. Use straight pin to place beads in area; allow to dry. Repeat for remaining outlined areas.
6. Use craft knife to cut pin and earrings from paper bag strips. Paint edges and backs of pin and earrings black; allow to dry. Apply two to three coats of sealer to pin and earrings; allow to dry. Glue pin and earring backs to jewelry; allow to dry.

HOLIDAY ACCENTS

The uses for these folksy painted ornaments are endless! Made from brown paper bags, our crafty padded accents will look great embellishing packages or dressing up a seasonal garland.

HOLIDAY PAPER BAG ORNAMENTS

Recycled items: large brown paper bags
You will also need batting, tracing paper, transfer paper, assorted colors of acrylic paint, paintbrushes, decorative-edge craft scissors, wire cutters, and medium-gauge craft wire.

Refer to Painting Techniques, page 156, before beginning project. Allow paint to dry after each application.

1. To prepare each bag, cut bag open along one fold; cut away and discard bottom. Press bag with a warm, dry iron.
2. For each ornament, cut one 10" square from batting and two 10" squares from bag. Trace desired pattern, pages 136 - 139, onto tracing paper. Use transfer paper to transfer design to unprinted side of one paper square. Paint design.
3. Place batting on printed side of remaining paper square. Place painted paper square right side up on batting. Using a short stitch length, machine stitch around design 1/8" from design. Use craft scissors to cut out ornament 1/8" outside sewn line.
4. Use wire cutters to cut a 12" length of craft wire. For hanger, work one end of wire through ornament; bend up and twist to secure. Curl 4" of wire at center around a pencil; remove pencil. Work remaining end of wire through ornament; bend up and twist to secure.

PLAYTIME PACK

here kids can be found, toys will abound! Our nifty backpack will make it easy to tote small treasures, and you can fashion it using ordinary brown paper bags. The star-spangled look is created with sponge-painting and buttons, and the straps are made with lengths of ribbon.

PLAY BACKPACK

Recycled items: two large brown paper bags
You will also need a hot glue gun; $^3/_4$" x 2" hook and loop fastener; spray adhesive; tracing paper; compressed craft sponge; white, red, and blue acrylic paint; black permanent medium-point marker; assorted white, red, and blue buttons; craft knife; cutting mat; and two 30" lengths of $1^1/_2$"w grosgrain ribbon.

Refer to Painting Techniques, page 156, before beginning project.

1. Draw a line $4^1/_2$" from top of one bag along one long side and each short side. Cut out bag along drawn lines. Draw a curved line on inside back of bag for flap (Fig. 1). Cut out flap along drawn line.

Fig. 1

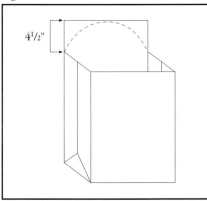

2. Glue loop side of fastener to inside of flap. Fold flap over to front of backpack. Aligning hook side of fastener with loop side of fastener, glue hook side of fastener to backpack.
3. Measure inside height and width of back of backpack. Cut a piece from remaining bag the determined measurements. Apply spray adhesive to one side of bag piece. For reinforcement, position and smooth bag piece inside back of backpack.
4. Trace star pattern, page 151, onto tracing paper; cut out. Draw around pattern on sponge; cut out shape. Sponge paint stars on flap and front of backpack. Use marker to add "stitches" around

stars. Arrange and glue buttons on flap and front of backpack.
5. Use craft knife to cut two $1^1/_2$"w diagonal slits $1^1/_2$" apart at top center back of backpack. Use craft knife to cut two $1^1/_2$"w slits 8" apart at bottom of backpack.
6. For each shoulder strap, thread end of ribbon through one slit at top of backpack; glue 2" to inside top of backpack. Thread remaining end of ribbon through one slit at bottom of backpack. Place backpack on child; adjust shoulder straps to fit. Mark placement of strap. Remove backpack from child. Glue strap inside bottom of backpack to secure.

PRETTY PANSIES

*F*or a vibrant accent for the front door or entry hall, craft our pansy wreath! Just cut the leaf and petal motifs from a brown paper bag; then paint them in bright colors. Attach the blooms to a grapevine wreath wrapped in pretty plaid ribbon for year-round appeal.

PANSY WREATH

Recycled item: large brown paper bag

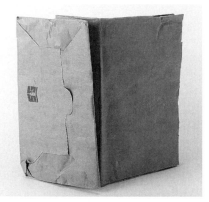

You will also need tracing paper; decorative-edge craft scissors; white spray primer; light green, green, dark green, black, and assorted colors of acrylic paint; assorted paintbrushes; matte acrylic spray sealer; drawing compass; craft glue; green chenille stem; hot glue gun; 1¼ yds. of 1½"w wired ribbon; 18" dia. grapevine wreath; wire cutters; floral wire; and 12" of 4"w wired ribbon.

Use craft glue for all gluing unless otherwise indicated. Allow primer, paint, sealer, and glue to dry after each application.

1. To prepare bag, cut bag open along one fold; cut away and discard bottom. Press bag with a warm, dry iron.

2. Trace patterns, page 150, onto tracing paper; cut out. Draw around leaf pattern five times on paper bag; use craft scissors to cut out shapes. Draw around small petal pattern twice and medium and large petal pattern four times each (two each in reverse) on paper bag; cut out shapes.

3. Apply primer to leaves and petals. Paint leaves dark green. Paint green veins on leaves. Paint petals desired color. Working from narrow end to wide end, use a stiff dry paintbrush to streak petals in a contrasting color. Paint black veins on small and medium petals. Paint tips of small petals black. Paint light green dots on tips of small petals. Apply two to three coats of sealer to leaves and petals.

4. For flower bases, use compass to draw two 2½" dia. circles on remainder of paper bag; cut out shapes. For each flower, beginning with large petals and overlapping as necessary, arrange and glue two large, two medium, then one small petal to one base.

5. Cut two 1" lengths from chenille stem. Bend each chenille piece into a "V" shape. Glue one shape to center of each flower.

6. For wreath, using hot glue to secure at each end, wrap 1½"w ribbon around wreath. For each leaf and flower, use wire cutters to cut an 8" length from floral wire. Bend wire length in half. Hot glue bend in wire to back of leaves and flowers. Use wire to attach leaves, then flowers to wreath.

7. For bow, press ends of 4"w ribbon ½" to wrong side; glue to secure. Knot ribbon at center. Glue knot to wreath.

QUILT-BLOCK CHARM

If you can sew on a button, you can make this charming quilt block wall hanging! The pretty pattern is simply cut from coordinating fabrics and fused to a backing crafted from brown paper sacks. Use a black permanent marker to create the "hand stitching."

WALL HANGING

Recycled items: four to five large brown paper bags

You will also need paper-backed fusible web, ³/₈ yd. of 45"w fabric for borders and centers, ¹/₈ yd. each of four coordinating fabrics for "quilt" pieces, black permanent medium-point marker, hot glue gun, embroidery floss to coordinate with buttons, and nine 1" dia. buttons.

1. To prepare each bag, cut bag open along one fold; cut away and discard bottom. Press bag with a warm, dry iron.
2. For wall hanging, cut two 24¹/₂" squares from paper bags, piecing as necessary. Cut a 24¹/₂" square from web. Fuse web to printed side of one bag piece. Matching printed sides, fuse paper bag pieces together.

3. Cut one 13¹/₂" x 26" piece each from fabric for border and web. Fuse web to wrong side of fabric piece. Cut fabric piece into six 1¹/₂" x 26" strips. Center and fuse strips along top, bottom, then side edges of wall hanging. For "blocks," center and fuse one strip vertically, then one strip horizontally to wall hanging. Trim ends of strips even with edges of wall hanging.
4. Use patterns, page 149, and follow *Making Appliqués,* page 157, to make four centers and 32 "quilt" pieces from fabrics.
5. Overlapping as necessary, arrange and fuse eight quilt pieces at center of each

block. Arrange and fuse centers on quilt pieces. Use marker to draw "stitches" along outer edges of quilt pieces.
6. For hanging loops, cut three 1¹/₂" x 7" strips from paper bag. Matching short ends, fold each strip in half to form loop; glue ends together. Spacing evenly across top, glue ends of hanging loops to back of wall hanging.
7. Beginning and ending at front and leaving a 5" tail of floss at each end, use embroidery floss to sew buttons to wall hanging. Knot floss ends together at front of wall hanging; trim ends.

SPIN THE BOTTLE

Is your recycling bin overflowing with bottles? Reclaim those handy extras with the clever ideas in this section! You'll find many wonderful ways to transform empties of all types into delightful decorator items. Who would guess the plucky little chicken perching on the kitchen counter had a former life as a gallon-sized plastic bottle? And just look at the beautiful "stained glass" hurricane lamp — it was once a common soda-pop container. For crafting projects both practical and whimsical, these instructions will help you put a new spin on old bottles.

RECYCLING QUEEN

This shimmering beauty is the queen of recycling! Sheathed in a gown of bubble wrap, she takes her shape from a plastic soda bottle. Her golden crown and curls, clipped from painted beverage cans, dress up a light-bulb head.

RECYCLE RITA

Recycled items: three 12-oz. aluminum beverage cans, twig, light bulb, nine metal bottle caps, 2-liter plastic soda bottle, 2"h x 4" dia. can, two lightweight metal forks, and bubble wrap

You will also need utility scissors; crimping tool; tracing paper; lightweight cardboard; garden clippers; low-temperature glue gun; white spray primer; white, gold, and copper spray paint; transfer paper; red and black acrylic paint; paintbrushes; household sponge; craft knife; cutting mat; 12" of medium-gauge craft wire; and household cement.

Allow primer, paint, and household cement to dry after each application. Use hot glue for all gluing unless otherwise indicated.

1. For crown, use utility scissors to cut through opening of one beverage can; cut away and discard top of can. Trim can to 1³/₄" from bottom of can. Beginning at cut edge and cutting to within ¹/₂" from bottom of can, cut a sawtooth pattern around can.

2. For hair, use utility scissors to cut through opening and down to bottom of two remaining beverage cans; cut away and discard tops and bottoms. Flatten can pieces. Cut can pieces into ³/₈" x 8¹/₂" strips. Use crimping tool to crimp strips.

3. For wand, trace star pattern, page 143, onto tracing paper; cut out. Draw around pattern on cardboard; cut out shape. Use garden clippers to cut a 10" length from twig. Glue star to one end of twig.

4. Apply two to three coats of primer to light bulb, bottle caps, bottle, can, and both sides of crown, hair pieces, and forks. Spray paint bottle caps, wand, and both sides of crown gold; both sides of hair pieces copper; and light bulb, bottle, forks, and can white.

5. For head, trace face pattern, page 143, onto tracing paper. Use transfer paper to transfer face to light bulb. Use acrylic paint to paint face. Lightly sponge paint eyelids, nose, cheeks, and chin red.

6. For body, mark around bottle 4" from top and 4¹/₂" from bottom. Use craft knife to cut slits at ¹/₂" intervals around bottle between lines (Fig. 1). Wrap wire around bottle at center of slits to form waist. Twist wire ends together.

Fig. 1

7. To assemble figurine, apply household cement to base of head; insert in bottle opening. Use household cement to glue hair, then crown to head; shape ends of hair and points of crown as desired.

8. For arms, use craft knife to make a slit in each side of top of bottle long enough to insert handle end of fork. Apply household cement to handle end of each fork; insert into slits.

9. For base, use household cement to glue bottom of bottle to closed end of can.

10. Trimming to fit and spot gluing to secure, wrap body and base with bubble wrap. Cut one 5" x 20" piece and one 3¹/₂" x 20" piece from bubble wrap. Overlapping ends at back, gather and glue one long edge of 5" x 20" piece of bubble wrap around waist and 3¹/₂" x 20" piece of bubble wrap around base.

11. For necklace, arrange and glue bottle caps around neck. Wrap tines of one fork around wand; use household cement to secure if necessary.

CREATIVE CANDLESTICKS

*P*erfect for a mantel, dining table, or nightstand, these elegant candlesticks are as simple to make as they are beautiful! Choose a crackle medium or tissue paper finish, or try one of each for a striking pair. Wrap the tops with ivy or berries for a delicate finale.

BOTTLE CANDLESTICKS

Recycled items: two 2-liter plastic soda bottles and two glass bottles, each with a 1" dia. mouth

You will also need a craft knife; cutting mat; hot glue gun; white, gold, and green acrylic paint; paintbrushes; crackle medium; white tissue paper; foam brush; craft glue; household sponge; and artificial gold berries or ivy for trim.

Refer to Painting Techniques, page 156, before beginning project. Allow paint and crackle medium to dry after each application.

1. For each candlestick, mark around one 2-liter bottle 1³/₄" from top. Use craft knife to cut top from 2-liter bottle; discard bottom of bottle. Hot glue threaded end of bottle piece inside mouth of desired glass bottle.

2. For crackled candlestick, paint inside top and outside of candlestick gold. Follow manufacturer's instructions to apply crackle medium to outside of candlestick. Paint outside of candlestick white.

3. For tissue paper-covered candlestick, lightly crumple tissue paper; smooth out. Trimming to fit, cut a piece of tissue paper large enough to cover inside top and outside of candlestick. Use foam brush to apply craft glue to inside top and outside of bottle. Smooth tissue paper onto candlestick; allow to dry. Paint candlestick green. Sponge paint candlestick gold.

4. Hot glue berries or ivy around each candlestick as desired.

SHORELINE TREASURE

Who says you have to live near the shore to enjoy its many treasures? Our inventive lamp begins as a plastic two-liter bottle that you fill with a colorful collection of seashells. Attach a lamp kit and a fabric-covered shade for a beautiful decorative finish.

SODA BOTTLE LAMP

Recycled item: 2-liter plastic bottle
You will also need a craft knife, cutting mat, seashells, clear cellophane tape, houschold cement, 4^1/$_2$" dia. Shaker box, hot glue gun, decorative trim, 1"w cork strip, lamp kit for bottle base, lampshade, tissue paper, fabric, and spray adhesive.

Use hot glue for all gluing unless otherwise indicated. Allow houschold cement to dry after each application.

1. Use craft knife to cut a 7^1/$_2$" long slit in back of bottle. Fill bottle with seashells. Tape opening closed.
2. Use household cement to glue bottom of bottle inside Shaker box. Trimming to fit, glue a length of trim around rim of Shaker box.
3. Trimming to fit, glue enough cork around thread pipe of lamp kit to enable lamp to fit securely in bottle opening. Follow manufacturer's instructions to assemble lamp.
4. Cut a 5^1/$_2$"l strip from cork. Use household cement to glue strip around top of bottle. Trimming to fit, glue a length of trim around each edge of cork strip.
5. Follow *Covering a Lampshade*, page 159, to cover lampshade with fabric. Trimming to fit, glue trim along top and bottom edge of lampshade.
6. Tear a 1^1/$_2$" x 18" strip from fabric. Tie fabric strip into a bow; notch ends. Glue bow to lampshade, then seashells to knot of bow.

Perfect for roosting on your countertop, this handy kitchen caddy will keep you from "scrambling" for your cooking utensils! No one would guess that our helpful hen's stuffed muslin body surrounds the bottom half of a gallon jug!

CHICKEN SPOON CADDY

Recycled item: 1-gallon plastic bottle

You will also need a craft knife, cutting mat, ³/₄ yd. of muslin, string, thumbtack, pencil, polyester fiberfill, hot glue gun, natural excelsior, tracing paper, ¹/₄ yd. each of gold and red fabric, straight pin, wooden skewer, soft sculpture needle, two ⁷/₈" dia. black buttons, cosmetic blush, and two 9" lengths of jute twine.

Match right sides and use a ¹/₄" seam allowance for all sewing. Allow glue to dry after each application.

1. Mark around bottle 7" from bottom. Use craft knife to cut top from bottle; discard top.

2. For body, cut a 22" square piece from muslin. Follow *Cutting a Fabric Circle*, page 159, and use 11" for string measurement to cut a circle from muslin to cover bottle piece. Leaving a 5" tail of thread at beginning and end, baste around circle ¹/₈" from edge. Place bottle piece in center of circle. Pull ends of thread to begin gathering muslin around edge of bottle. Fill space between bottle and muslin with desired amount of fiberfill. Pull ends of thread to tighten muslin around top edge of bottle; knot thread ends to secure, then trim ends. Adjust gathers as necessary; spot glue to secure. Fill bottle with excelsior.

3. Trace patterns, pages 146 and 147, onto tracing paper; cut out. Using patterns, cut two heads and four each of wings and feet from muslin; two combs and two wattles from red fabric; and two beaks from gold fabric. Cut two 3" x 20" strips from gold fabric for legs. Cut one 2" x 18" and one 3" x 18" piece from gold fabric for collar.

4. For head, sew along two edges of beak. Turn beak right side out. Lightly stuff beak with fiberfill. Matching raw edges, pin beak to right side of one head piece where indicated on pattern. Leaving bottom open, sew head pieces together. Turn head right side out. Leaving a 5" tail of thread at beginning and end, baste around bottom of head ¹/₈" from edge. Stuff head with fiberfill. Insert skewer in bottom of head. Pull thread ends to tightly gather bottom of head around skewer; knot thread ends to secure, then trim ends. Glue skewer to inside of bottle to secure.

5. Leaving an opening for turning, sew comb pieces together. Turn comb right side out. Stuff comb with fiberfill. Sew opening closed. Leaving an opening for turning, sew wattle pieces together. Turn wattle right side out. Stuff wattle with fiberfill. Sew opening closed. Glue comb and wattle to head. Use soft sculpture needle to sew on buttons for eyes. Apply blush for cheeks.

6. For collar, with right sides up and aligning one long edge, place 2" x 18" collar piece on top of 3" x 18" collar piece. Leaving a 5" tail of thread at beginning and end, baste along aligned edges. Clip collar pieces at ¹/₂" intervals to ¹/₄" from basting threads. Place collar around neck. Pull thread ends to tightly gather collar around neck; knot thread ends to secure, then trim ends.

7. For each wing, leaving an opening for turning, sew two wing pieces together. Turn wing right side out. Stuff wing with fiberfill. Sew opening closed. Glue wings to sides of body.

8. For each leg, matching long edges, fold one strip in half. Sew along long edges of strip. Turn right side out. Thread one length of twine through strip. Sewing at open ends to secure, gather strip to fit twine.

9. For each foot, leaving an opening for turning, sew two feet pieces together. Turn foot right side out. Stuff foot with fiberfill. Sew opening closed. Glue feet to ends of legs. Glue opposite ends of legs to body.

PICNIC PLEASER

*O*f the many warm-weather pleasures to be enjoyed, picnics and barbecues are perennial favorites! Add a bright touch of summertime color to your outdoor gatherings with this cute utensil caddy made from one-gallon bottles. It's so easy to create, you might want to make extras to hold additional napkins and condiments!

UTENSIL CADDY

Recycled items: two 1-gallon plastic bottles

You will also need a craft knife, cutting mat, fabric, spray adhesive, hot glue gun, white rattail cord, hammer, nail, and 10" of medium-gauge craft wire.

1. Mark around each bottle 6" from bottom. Use craft knife to cut tops from bottles; discard tops. Cut a $1^1/2$"w ring from one bottle bottom; discard remainder of bottle bottom. Cut across ring to make a strip.
2. For basket, measure around bottle bottom; add 1". Cut a piece from fabric 9" by the determined measurement. Press one short end of fabric $1/4$" to wrong side. Apply spray adhesive to outside and bottom of basket. With 1" of fabric extending beyond top of basket and pressed edge overlapping raw edge at back, smooth fabric around basket. Glue pressed edge to basket to secure. Pleating as necessary, glue excess fabric to inside and onto bottom of basket.
3. For handle, measure width of strip; add 2". Measure length of strip; add 2". Cut a piece from fabric the determined measurements. Apply spray adhesive to wrong side of fabric piece. Overlapping as necessary, smooth fabric around strip.
4. Trimming to fit, hot glue cord around basket $1/8$" from top and along each long edge of handle.
5. Measuring $3/8$" from top, use hammer and nail to punch two holes 1" apart on one side of basket; repeat for opposite side of basket.
6. To attach handle at each side, cut one 14" length from cord. Wrap wire around one end of cord length. Aligning holes in handle end with holes in basket and working from outside to inside, thread wire and cord through one set of holes. Leaving a $6^1/2$" long tail of cord on outside, thread wire and cord back through remaining set of holes. Tie cord ends into a bow on outside of basket. Knot cord ends, then trim. Repeat to attach opposite end of handle.

BEAUTIFUL BAG LADY

*D*on't waste valuable storage space on those useful but unsightly plastic bags — let this sweet miss mind them for you! Made from child-size socks and a two-liter bottle, this holder puts a fresh face on recycling while adding a bit of fun to your kitchen or pantry.

RECYCLE DOLLY

Recycled items: 2-liter plastic bottle and three child-size socks with eyelet ruffles

You will also need a craft knife, cutting mat, tea bag, polyester fiberfill, hot glue gun, two ¼" dia. buttons for eyes, red permanent medium-point marker, fabric, ½"w fusible web tape, safety pin, 9" of ¼"w elastic, 30" of ¼"w grosgrain ribbon, curly doll hair, artificial flowers, and a 6½" dia. straw hat including brim.

Match wrong sides and raw edges and use a ¼" seam allowance for all sewing unless otherwise indicated.

1. Mark around bottle 2½" from bottom. Use craft knife to cut bottom from bottle; discard bottom.
2. Follow *Tea Dyeing*, page 156, to dye socks.
3. For head, stuff toe of sock to form a 3" dia. ball. Tie a length of thread tightly

around sock below stuffing. Folding cuff to right side and with ruffle gathered around bottom of head, place head in top of bottle. Glue to secure. Glue eyes to head. Use marker to draw mouth.
4. For dress, cut a 20" x 23" piece from fabric. Sew long sides together to form a tube. For casing at bottom of dress, press

one raw edge ¼" to wrong side. Press 1" to wrong side again. Leaving an opening at seam to insert elastic, sew along edge of first pressed edge. Sew ¾" from stitched line to form casing. Use safety pin to thread elastic through casing. Sew ends of elastic together. Sew opening in casing closed.
5. For neck edge of dress, press remaining raw edge ¼" to wrong side; press ¼" to wrong side again. Stitch in place. Turn dress right side out. Leaving a 5" tail at each end, baste around neck edge of dress. Matching neck edge of dress with neck of bottle, place bottle in dress. Pull thread ends to gather dress tightly around neck of bottle; knot ends together.
6. For each arm, measuring from toe, stuff 5" of sock. Tightly tie a length of thread around sock below stuffing. Fold cuff of sock to right side with edge of ruffle 2" from toe.
7. For each sleeve, cut a 4½" x 5" piece from fabric. Press each long edge ¼" to wrong side; press ¼" to wrong side again. Stitch in place. Sew remaining raw edges together to form a tube. Turn sleeve right side out. Insert arm in sleeve. Blind stitch one end of sleeve to arm above ruffle. Gather and tack remaining end to side of dress at neck of bottle.
8. Glue hair to top of head. Tear two ¾" x 10" strips from fabric. For ponytails, gather hair at each side of head. Tie one fabric strip around each ponytail to secure.
9. Glue flowers to hat, then hat to head.
10. For hanger and neck ties, fold ribbon in half. Leaving 8" streamers for neck ties, knot ribbon ends together to form hanging loop. Glue knot to hat brim at back. Tie streamers into a bow around neck.

TEACHER'S TREAT

*Y*our child's favorite teacher is sure to appreciate a shiny "apple" filled with yummy treats! It's a cinch to create this cheery canister using bottoms cut from two-liter plastic bottles. Just spray paint the pieces and add a twig stem. A strip of alphabet-print fabric and a chalkboard gift tag add folksy style to the fun offering.

APPLE TREAT HOLDER

Recycled items: two 2-liter plastic soda bottles and a twig

You will also need a craft knife, cutting mat, red spray paint, fabric, craft glue, household cement, garden clippers, two artificial leaves, and a miniature chalkboard ornament.

Use household cement for all gluing unless otherwise indicated. Allow paint, craft glue, and household cement to dry after each application.

1. For top of treat holder, measuring 2¹/₄" from bottom, draw a line around one bottle. For bottom of treat holder, measuring 3" from bottom, draw a line around remaining bottle. Use craft knife to cut bottles along drawn lines. Cut a 1"w ring from top section of one bottle. Cut across ring to make strip. Discard remaining top sections.

2. Spray paint outsides of top and bottom of treat holder and one side of strip red.

3. Cut a ⁷/₈" x 14" strip from fabric. Overlapping ends at back, use craft glue to glue fabric strip around edge of bottom of treat holder.

4. With unpainted side facing inside, overlapping ends as necessary, and with ¹/₂" extending above cut edge, glue strip around inside of bottom of treat holder. Place top of treat holder over bottom of treat holder.

5. For stem, use garden clippers to cut a ³/₄"l twig. Glue leaves, then stem to top of treat holder. Hang ornament on stem.

56

MAJESTIC MOSAIC

*D*on't trash that empty soda bottle — we've discovered a way to transform it into a gorgeous home accent! This colorful hurricane lamp is simple to make: just cover the inside of a two-liter bottle section with tissue paper, and paint in rich colors. Outline the sections with glittery paint for a majestic look.

HURRICANE GLOBE

Recycled item: 2-liter plastic bottle
You will also need a craft knife, cutting mat, white tissue paper, decoupage glue, foam brush, grease pencil, assorted colors of acrylic paint, paintbrushes, paper towel, and gold dimensional paint.

1. Mark around bottle 4" from top and 1³/₄" from bottom. Use craft knife to cut top and bottom from bottle; discard top and bottom.
2. Lightly crumple tissue paper; smooth out. Cut a piece from tissue paper large enough to cover inside of bottle piece.
3. Mix one part glue with one part water. Use foam brush to apply glue mixture to inside of bottle piece. Smooth tissue paper piece on inside of bottle piece; allow to dry.
4. Use grease pencil to draw desired shapes on outside of bottle piece.
5. For each paint color, mix one part acrylic paint with one part water. Paint tissue side of each shape as desired; allow to dry.
6. Use paper towel to remove grease pencil. Working on outside of bottle piece, use dimensional paint to outline shapes and top and bottom of bottle piece; allow to dry.

PATIO LANTERN

For soft evening light, hang this intriguing accent on your porch or patio! Glass beads shine, while vine-like wire tendrils add a rustic touch. The shadows cast by the flickering candles add an air of mystery to the natural shape of the driftwood hanger.

Recycled items: newspaper, three single-serving glass beverage bottles, candle pieces, large can, and a 30" long piece of driftwood

You will also need a saucepan, craft stick, oven mitt, three candles to fit in bottles, wire cutters, heavy-gauge craft wire, assorted glass beads, craft drill, wood glue, three eye screws, and three "S" hooks.

Do not melt candle pieces over an open flame or in a pan placed directly on burner.

1. Wash and thoroughly dry each bottle.
2. To melt wax, cover work area with newspaper. Adding water as necessary, heat 1" of water in a saucepan to boiling. Place candle pieces in large can. Pinch top of can to form a spout. Place can in boiling water; reduce heat to a simmer. Stir with craft stick if necessary.
3. Using an oven mitt, carefully pour wax in each bottle to a depth of $^1/_2$". Allow wax to harden slightly. Insert one candle in each bottle. Allow wax to harden completely.

4. For each bottle hanger, use wire cutters to cut a 22" long piece of wire. Leaving a $2^1/_2$" tail of wire, wrap one end of wire around neck of bottle; bend tail of wire up and twist to secure. If desired, curl tail of wire around a pencil; remove pencil. Thread beads onto wire as desired. Form wire into a U-shape over opening of bottle. Leaving a $2^1/_2$" tail of wire, thread remaining end of wire under wire on opposite side of bottle neck; bend tail of wire up and twist to secure. If desired, curl tail of wire around a pencil; remove pencil.
5. Drill three pilot holes in driftwood as desired for placement of bottles. Apply glue to threaded end of each eye screw. Screw one eye screw into each pilot hole in driftwood; allow glue to dry.
6. Use wire cutters to cut three lengths from wire at least 6" long. Leaving a tail of wire, thread one end of each wire length through one eye screw; bend tail of each wire up and twist to secure. If desired, curl tail of each wire around a pencil; remove pencil. Thread beads onto each wire as desired. Thread remaining end of each length of wire around one side of one "S" hook. Hang one bottle from each "S" hook.
7. For driftwood hanger, use wire cutters to cut two one-yard lengths of wire. Twist wire lengths together. Wrap ends of wire lengths around ends of drift wood. Use wire cutters to cut various lengths of wire. If desired, curl wire lengths around a pencil; remove pencil. Thread beads onto wire lengths as desired. Bend and twist wire lengths around hanger to secure.

CARD TRICKS

It's doubly difficult to throw out old greeting cards . . . both because of their beauty and because of the sweet sentiments attached! Now you can have your card and recycle it, too! We've found more than a dozen great ways to display and reuse these miniature works of art, from small gift items to refurbished furniture. You can create a beautiful frame, a handy bookmark, or a breathtaking hurricane lamp. Perhaps you'd prefer to enhance a lampshade or embellish a pretty plate? Whichever project you choose, it's time to break out the scissors and glue; then pick a card, any card — and make recycling magic!

61

PASTEL POSIES

Greeting cards are like little pieces of art, so don't toss them — use them to make something beautiful! Cover an ordinary photo album with pastel card stock; then cut motifs from the cards to create a collage. The only thing more special than the album will be the photos inside!

PHOTO ALBUM

Recycled items: greeting cards
You will also need a 5" x 8½" photo album with a removable plastic cover; yellow, pink, and blue card stock; and a craft glue stick.

Allow glue to dry after each application.

1. Remove plastic cover from album.
2. Measure height and width of album spine; add ¼" to width measurement. Cut one piece from pink card stock the determined measurements. Overlapping onto front and back of album, glue card stock piece to spine of album.
3. Measure height of front of album; add 1½". Measure width of front of album; add ¾". Cut one piece each from yellow and blue card stock the determined measurements. With ¾" of card stock piece extending beyond top, bottom, and open edge of album, glue blue card stock piece to front of album. Clipping as necessary, fold card stock to inside of album; spot glue to secure. Repeat to cover back of album with yellow card stock piece.
4. Cut desired motifs from cards. Arrange and glue motifs on spine and on front of album.
5. Replace plastic cover on album.

SWEET SENTIMENTS

*N*othing is more treasured than a special accent you make yourself, and this sentimental wreath is no exception! Use discarded costume jewelry and greeting card cutouts to decorate a purchased twig wreath; then give it a heartwarming feel with old family photographs.

WREATH

Recycled items: greeting cards and costume jewelry pieces
You will also need a hot glue gun, desired photographs, 14" dia. twig wreath, and 22" of 1¹/₂"w wired ribbon.

1. Cut desired motifs from cards.
2. Arrange motifs, photographs, and jewelry pieces on wreath; glue to secure.
3. Tie ribbon into a bow; notch ends. Glue bow to wreath.

POSIE PAGE MINDERS

Why not turn those "too-pretty-to-throw-away" greeting cards into terrific ribbon bookmarks! Cut out motifs, glue to ribbon lengths, and trim with lace, rickrack, and assorted jewel stones for a feminine look.

RIBBON BOOKMARKS

Recycled items: greeting cards
You will also need assorted ribbons, craft glue, decorative trims (we used rickrack and flat lace), and assorted acrylic jewels.

Allow glue to dry after each application.

1. Cut an 11¹/₂" length from desired ribbon. Trim ribbon ends as desired.
2. Trimming to fit, glue trim along edges of ribbon.
3. Cut desired motifs from cards. Arrange and glue motifs at each end of ribbon. Glue jewels to motifs as desired.

KEEPSAKE MEMORIES

*G*ot a drawer or box full of greeting cards that are just too dear to toss? Preserve them on memory pages! It's so easy to create these beautiful keepsakes, you'll want to make enough to fill an album.

CARD MEMORY PAGES

Recycled items: greeting cards
You will also need straight-edge scissors, assorted decorative-edge craft scissors, decorative papers, decorative items to embellish pages (we used paper doilies), desired photographs, scrapbook pages, craft glue stick, and a black permanent medium-point marker.

1. Use craft scissors to cut motifs from cards and shapes from decorative papers.
2. Arrange motifs, paper pieces, decorative items, and photographs on pages; glue in place.
3. Use marker to write names, dates, or messages and add details to pages.

EASY ELEGANCE

*E*very bit as lovely as the ones found in expensive gift shops, these pretty soaps won't put a strain on your pocketbook! Using motifs cut from greeting cards, you can decoupage ordinary bars of soap to add elegance to a guest bathroom.

EMBELLISHED SOAPS

Recycled items: floral-motif greeting cards

You will also need a foam brush, decoupage glue, and bars of soap.

Soaps are for decorative use only.

1. For each bar of soap, cut desired motifs from cards.
2. Use foam brush to apply glue to backs of motifs. Arrange motifs on soap and smooth in place; allow to dry.
3. Allowing to dry between each coat, apply two coats of glue over motifs.

ROSY GLOW

*C*andles used as decorative accents are more popular than ever! Here's a quick way to create a beautiful pillar with little or no expense at all. Simply decoupage greeting card cutouts to a new candle, or use the motifs to cover imperfections on an old one!

DECOUPAGED CANDLE

Recycled items: lid from 6½" dia. tin for stand and greeting cards

You will also need white spray paint, decorative napkin, spray adhesive, foam brush, craft glue, 4" dia. x 9" h pillar candle, 12" of 2"w sheer ribbon, and a hot glue gun.

1. Spray paint stand white; allow to dry.
2. Separate plies of napkin. Cut a piece from napkin large enough to cover stand. Apply spray adhesive to stand. Smooth napkin piece onto stand; glue edges to inside of stand.
3. Cut desired motifs from cards. Use foam brush to apply craft glue to backs of motifs. Position and smooth motifs onto candle and stand; allow to dry.
4. Place candle on stand. Tie ribbon into a bow. Hot glue bow to stand.

BRIGHT LITTLE SHADE

*J*azz up an ordinary candlestick lamp with this cute lampshade! Cut motifs from greeting cards to decorate the shade; then add rickrack and a ribbon bow for a cheery finishing touch.

CARD-EMBELLISHED LAMPSHADE

Recycled items: greeting cards
You will also need a foam brush, craft glue, lampshade, assorted colors of rickrack, and 7" of ¼"w satin ribbon.

Allow glue to dry after each application.

1. Cut desired motifs from cards. Use foam brush to apply glue to backs of motifs. Arrange and smooth motifs on lampshade.
2. Trimming to fit, glue rickrack around top and bottom edges of lampshade. Tie ribbon into a bow. Glue bow to lampshade.

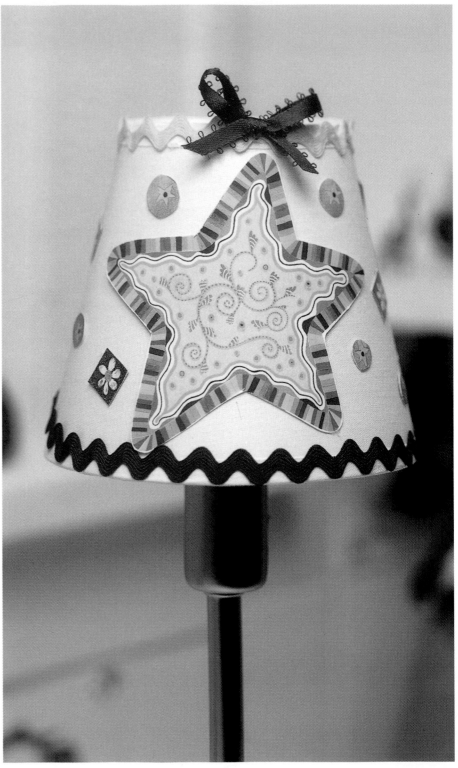

ARTSY ACCENT TABLE

Here's a great project for showing off your artistic style! Simply cut motifs from greeting cards and decoupage them on the painted top of a round table. A skirt of gathered fabric gives a tailored finish to this eye-catching accent.

DECOUPAGED ROUND TABLE

Recycled items: greeting cards
You will also need white spray paint, round table, foam brush, decoupage glue, fabric, hot glue gun, and 1"w grosgrain ribbon.

Use decoupage glue for all gluing unless otherwise indicated.

1. Spray paint tabletop white; allow to dry.
2. Cut desired motifs from cards. Use foam brush to apply glue to backs of motifs. Arrange and smooth motifs on tabletop; allow to dry. Apply glue over motifs; allow to dry.
3. For table skirt, measure height of table; add 2". Measure around tabletop; multiply by 2½. Cut a piece from fabric the determined measurements, piecing as necessary. Press each long edge of fabric piece ½" to wrong side; press ½" to wrong side again and stitch in place. Leaving a 5" tail of thread at each end, baste along one long edge. With basted edge along edge of tabletop, place fabric piece around tabletop. Pull basting threads to gather fabric to fit around tabletop. Distributing gathers evenly around table, hot glue gathers along side of tabletop.
4. Trimming to fit, hot glue ribbon around skirt ½" from edge of tabletop. Cut an 18" length of ribbon; tie into a bow. Notch ribbon ends. Hot glue bow to ribbon at front of table.

GARDEN GREETING

*G*reet garden visitors with a charming sign crafted from wooden paint stirrers and floral cutouts! Paint on a heartwarming message for an extra burst of sunshine.

GARDEN GATE SIGN

Recycled items: floral-motif greeting cards

You will also need four paint stirrers; hot glue gun; two craft sticks; ivory, green, and brown acrylic paint; paintbrushes; glazing medium; foam brushes; paper towels; tracing paper; transfer paper; polyurethane spray sealer; craft glue; and jute twine.

Allow paint and sealer to dry after each application unless otherwise indicated. Use hot glue for all gluing unless otherwise indicated.

1. For sign back, leaving 1/8" between paint stirrers, arrange paint stirrers horizontally on a flat surface. Leaving 5" between craft sticks, glue craft sticks across paint stirrers (Fig. 1).

Fig. 1

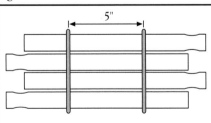

2. Apply two coats of ivory paint to front and back of sign.
3. Follow manufacturer's instructions to mix glazing medium with brown paint. Use foam brush to apply mixture to sign. Use paper towels to wipe away excess; allow to dry.

4. Trace design, page 134, onto tracing paper. Use transfer paper to transfer design to front of sign. Paint design green.
5. Cut desired motifs from greeting cards. Use craft glue to glue cutouts to sides of sign; allow to dry. Mix one part craft glue with one part water. Use foam brush to apply glue mixture to cutouts; allow to dry. Apply two to three coats of sealer to sign.
6. For hanger, cut a 24" length of twine; knot 3" from each end. Glue knots to back of sign.

NATURAL FLOWERPOT

*B*ring the look of the outdoors into your home with a beautiful decoupaged flowerpot. The earthy look is achieved with spatter painting and antiquing. We used leaf motifs cut from greeting cards to give it a natural feel.

DECOUPAGED FLOWERPOT

Recycled items: greeting cards
You will also need ecru spray paint, 6" dia. clay flowerpot, green and brown acrylic paint, toothbrush, foam brushes, decoupage glue, antiquing stain, and clear acrylic spray sealer.

Refer to Painting Techniques, page 156, before beginning project. Allow paint and sealer to dry after each application.

1. Spray paint inside and outside of flowerpot ecru. Spatter paint inside and outside of flowerpot green.
2. Cut desired motifs from cards. Use foam brush to apply glue to backs of motifs. Arrange and smooth motifs onto flowerpot; allow to dry.
3. Follow *Antiquing*, page 157, to apply stain to flowerpot.
4. Apply two to three coats of sealer to flowerpot.

PHOTO PIZZAZZ

*D*isplay your favorite photos with pizzazz! These refrigerator magnet frames are super-simple to make from old greeting cards (you know, the ones you have stuffed in drawers and boxes). Embellish the frames with satin ribbons; then add magnetic strips and fill the frames with your treasured photographs.

MAGNETIC CARD FRAMES

Recycled items: greeting cards
You will also need a craft knife, cutting mat, hot glue gun, desired photographs, assorted satin ribbons, and a craft magnetic sheet.

1. For each frame, use craft knife to cut desired portion from front of card (we left a flower intact on one of our cards).
2. Leaving an opening at top to insert photograph, glue remaining outer edges of card together. Insert photograph into card.
3. Cut a 6" length from ribbon. Tie ribbon into a bow. Glue bow to frame. Cut a 1¹/₂" x 2" piece from magnetic sheet. Glue magnet to back of frame.

SOMETHING TO TALK ABOUT

*Y*ou'll never have to hunt for
a phone number again with this
stylish directory. Cut floral motifs
from greeting cards to embellish a
painted wooden shutter; then label
the slats with all your frequently
used phone numbers. A garland of
greenery lends garden charm to
the resourceful decoration.

SHUTTER PHONE DIRECTORY

Recycled items: floral-motif greeting
cards

You will also need white acrylic paint,
paintbrush, hinged wooden shutter, foam
brush, decoupage glue, black permanent
fine-point marker, 1" x 3" self-adhesive
labels, hot glue gun, and an artificial ivy
garland.

1. Mix one part paint with one part water.
Paint shutter frame and slats; allow to dry.
2. Cut desired motifs from cards. Use
foam brush to apply decoupage glue to
backs of motifs. Arrange and smooth
motifs on shutter frame; allow to dry.
3. Use marker to write desired names and
telephone numbers on labels. Apply labels
to shutter slats.
4. Beginning and ending at bottom of
shutter and trimming to fit, hot glue
garland along sides and across top of
shutter.

CUSTOM FRAME-UP

*I*t's a snap to make your own picture frame . . . simply embellish a precut photo mat with greeting card motifs and other trims. We used florals for a sweet old-fashioned look, but you can customize yours any way you choose!

CARD CUTOUT FRAME

Recycled items: floral-motif greeting cards

You will also need craft glue, flat lace trim, 8" x 10" mat with a precut opening, craft knife, cutting mat, foam core board, and desired photograph.

Allow craft glue to dry after each application.

1. Trimming to fit, glue lace trim around edges of mat.
2. Cut desired motifs from cards. Use foam brush to apply glue to backs of motifs. Arrange and smooth motifs on mat; allow to dry.
3. For each dimensional cutout, cut desired motif from card. Use craft knife to cut piece from foam core board slightly smaller than motif. Glue foam core piece to back of motif.
4. Arrange and glue dimensional cutouts on mat.
5. Mount photograph in mat opening.

"SCENT-SATIONAL" SACHET

A *"scent-sational" gift, this pretty sachet is easy to make using greeting card motifs and a pocket cut from poster board! A tulle window allows the fragrance to escape.*

POTPOURRI HOLDER

Recycled items: greeting cards with floral motifs

You will also need tracing paper, transfer paper, poster board, craft knife, cutting mat, hot glue gun, $3^{1}/_{4}$" x $4^{1}/_{4}$" piece of tulle, scissors, potpourri, $8^{1}/_{2}$" of $2^{3}/_{4}$"w satin ribbon, foam brush, and decoupage glue.

1. Trace holder pattern, page 148, onto tracing paper. Enlarge pattern 200% on copier. Use transfer paper to transfer pattern, fold lines, and grey lines to one side (outside) of poster board. Cut out holder along outside lines.

2. For window, use craft knife to cut a 2" x 4" piece from center of holder. Center and glue tulle over opening on inside of holder.

3. Use one point of scissors to score holder along fold lines and grey lines shown on pattern. Overlapping at back, fold then glue sides of holder together.

4. Overlapping top over bottom, glue end flaps closed at one end. Fill holder with potpourri. Glue flaps of remaining end closed.

5. Press each end of ribbon $^{1}/_{4}$" to wrong side. Glue one end of ribbon at one end of window. Wrap ribbon around back of holder. Glue remaining end of ribbon to opposite end of window.

6. Cut desired motifs from cards. Use foam brush to apply decoupage glue to backs of motifs. Arrange and smooth motifs on holder; allow to dry.

FLOWERS AND CANDLELIGHT

T ransform an ordinary hurricane globe into a gorgeous home accent using items you might ordinarily throw away! Simply glue a motif cut from an old greeting card inside the globe and sponge paint the glass. Make the base using a painted can accented with another card design. A votive candle adds a warm glow.

HURRICANE GLOBE

Recycled items: greeting cards and a 1¹/₂"h x 3¹/₄" dia. can

You will also need a foam brush, decoupage glue, glass hurricane globe, ecru and green acrylic paint, sea sponges, white spray primer, paintbrushes, craft glue, decorative trim, votive, and a glass votive cup.

Refer to Painting Techniques, page 156, before beginning project. Use decoupage glue for all gluing unless otherwise indicated. Allow paint, primer, and craft glue to dry after each application.

1. For hurricane globe, cut desired motif from card. Use foam brush to apply decoupage glue to right side of motif.

Arrange and smooth motif inside globe; allow to dry. Sponge paint inside of globe ecru.

2. For base, apply primer to can. Paint can green. Sponge paint can ecru. Cut desired motif from card. Use foam brush to apply decoupage glue to wrong side of motif. Arrange and smooth motif below rim of can; allow to dry. Trimming to fit, use craft glue to glue trim to rim of can.

3. With votive in cup, place cup in center of base. Place hurricane globe in base.

DRESSED-UP DINNERWARE

*D*ress up the dinner table for a special occasion with custom-designed plates. Use decoupage glue to apply artificial leaves and greeting-card motifs to a clear plate; then spray the back with white paint. What a lovely way to personalize each place setting!

DECOUPAGED PLATE

Recycled items: floral-motif greeting cards

You will also need a foam brush, decoupage glue, 8" dia. clear glass plate, artificial leaves, off-white spray paint, and water-based satin polyurethane sealer.

1. Cut desired motifs from cards.
2. Use foam brush to apply glue to right sides of motifs. Working on back of plate, arrange and smooth motifs on plate; allow to dry. Use foam brush to apply glue to right sides of leaves. Working on back of plate, arrange and smooth leaves on plate; allow to dry.
3. Spray paint back of plate off-white; allow to dry. Follow manufacturer's instructions to apply two to three coats of sealer to back of plate.

SIMPLY "SOCK-SATIONAL"

Wondering what to do with those odd socks — the ones you keep leaving in the laundry hamper in the hope their mates will show up someday? How about refashioning that piece of forlorn footwear into a cute and cuddly doll or a handsome hobby horse! Or perhaps you'd like to alter an argyle to make a soothing microwaveable neck warmer or a handy draft dodger to chase the winter chill. You can even appliqué sock cutouts onto an old denim vest to extend the life of a wonderful wearable. In this section, you'll find a number of resourceful ways to reuse that solitary sock . . . without a lot of fancy footwork!

PINT-SIZE PLAYMATE

Precious in ponytails, this pretty pint-size pixie is the perfect playmate for your little princess. The adorable doll is sewn from an assortment of socks, and her luxurious curls are created by unraveling an old sweater! She's sure to inspire lots of hugs.

SOCK DOLL

Recycled items: adult-size white tube sock, child-size white sock, knitted solid-color sweater, adult-size solid-color sock, two child-size solid-color socks, and a knitted print sweater

You will also need polyester fiberfill, white and red embroidery floss, 12" of $7/8$"w ribbon, hot glue gun, two $1/2$" dia. black buttons for eyes, cosmetic blush, brown permanent fine-point marker, and doll socks and shoes for an 18" doll.

Refer to Embroidery Stitches, page 158, before beginning project. Use six strands of floss for all embroidery.

1. For legs, cut down center of cuff of tube sock through both thicknesses to end of ribbing. For head and body, stuff sock with fiberfill to legs. Sew cut edges of legs together. Stuff legs with fiberfill. Sew openings closed. For neck, tie a length of white floss around body.

2. For arms, measuring $5^1/2$" from toe, cut across child-size white sock; discard cuff portion of sock. Cut toe portion in half from cut edge to toe. Leaving an opening for stuffing, sew along cut edges. Stuff arms with fiberfill. Sew openings closed. Position and sew arms to body.

3. For hair, unravel yarn from solid-color sweater. Without stretching strands, cut several 24" yarn lengths. Securely sew center of each strand to top of head. Gather hair at each side of head for ponytails; tie a length of white floss around each ponytail to secure.

4. Measuring from toe, cut a 4" piece from adult-size solid-color sock for hat; set remainder of sock aside. Roll cut edge up. Place hat on head; tack at each side and at back to secure. Tie ribbon into a bow. Glue bow to hat.

5. Sew eyes to head. Pinch a small area on head for nose; whipstitch to secure. Use red floss to work one long *Straight Stitch* for mouth, then work one *French Knot* on each side of mouth. Apply blush for cheeks. Use marker to add freckles to cheeks.

6. Measuring from edge of cuff, cut a $3^3/4$" piece from remainder of adult-size solid-color sock. Roll cut end $1/8$" to outside. Fold cuff end $1/4$" to outside twice. Place sock piece on body for front and back of sweater. For sleeves, cut across toe end of each child-size solid-color sock; discard toe portion. With cut end at shoulder, place one sleeve on each arm. Gathering as necessary, sew sleeves to body and sweater. Fold cuff of each sleeve up $1/2$".

7. For skirt, cutting through all layers, cut a $4^1/2$" long piece from sleeve of print sweater. Press each cut edge $1/4$" to wrong side. Sew along one pressed edge for hem of skirt. Beginning and ending at center back and leaving a 5" tail at each end, work *Running Stitches* along remaining pressed edge. Place skirt on doll. Pull thread ends to gather skirt around waist; knot to secure. Trim thread ends.

8. Place socks and shoes on doll.

"DOGGONE" CUTE

*W*ho'd have thought dressing up your window could be so much "doggone" fun! Our winsome sock puppy sports felt features. Team him with canine-motif curtains for added fun!

DOGGIE WINDOW TREATMENT

Recycled items: adult-size white sock for each dog

You will also need polyester fiberfill; tracing paper; white, pink, and black felt; craft glue; white embroidery floss; bandanna, and 12" of floral wire.

Allow glue to dry after each application.

1. Stuff sock with fiberfill. Sew edges of cuff together. Tack toe of sock to cuff. For mouth, pinch two folds $^{1}/_{2}$"w apart in toe area of sock; tack folds together.
2. Trace patterns, page 154, onto tracing paper; cut out. Using patterns, cut one nose; two ears, eyebrows, pupils, and eyes; and six freckles from black felt. Cut two irises and six spots from white felt. Cut one tongue from pink felt.
3. Pinch a $^{1}/_{4}$"w pleat in base of each ear; tack to secure. Glue spots on ears. Glue ears on dog.

4. Layer and glue eye pieces together. Use three strands of floss to work *Straight Stitches*, page 158, for eye highlights. Glue eyebrows and eyes on dog.
5. Glue nose on dog. Glue three freckles on each side of nose. Glue tongue inside pleat for mouth.

6. Cut bandanna in half diagonally. Knot one half of bandanna around dog's "neck." Use wire to attach dog to end of a curtain rod.

WIGGLE WORM

*T*his whimsical "wiggle worm" is the solution to those drafty windows and doors! Salvage the cuffs from mismatched or worn socks, sew them together, and stuff. A foam ball forms the head, and pom-poms adorn the chenille-stem antennae. Glue on button accents just for fun!

SOCK DRAFT DODGER

Recycled items: nine adult-size socks
You will also need polyester fiberfill, 4" dia. plastic foam ball, 13" of $^3/_8$"w ribbon, tracing paper, transfer paper, white craft foam, black permanent medium-point marker, low-temperature glue gun, two bump chenille stems, two 1$^1/_4$" dia. pom-poms, assorted buttons, and a $^7/_8$" dia. bell.

1. For body, cut 4$^1/_2$" to 5$^1/_2$" long tubes from cuffs of eight socks; discard remaining portion of each sock. Sew cuff pieces together end to end to form one tube. Sew one end of tube closed. Stuff body with fiberfill.

2. For head, place plastic foam ball in toe of remaining sock. Stuff sock with fiberfill. For neck, tie ribbon into a bow around sock at bottom of head. Sew head to body.
3. Trace eyes pattern, page 151, onto tracing paper. Use transfer paper to transfer eyes to craft foam. Use marker to outline eyes. Cut out eyes. Glue eyes to head. Use marker to draw eyebrows and mouth on head.
4. For each antenna, cut a two-bump piece from one chenille stem. Work one end of antenna into head. Glue one pom-pom to remaining end of antenna.
5. Glue buttons to body as desired. Sew bell to tail.

AN APPLE FOR THE SEAMSTRESS

*A*ny seamstress will appreciate this cute country accessory. Starting with a child-size sock, it's so easy to create a stuffed apple-shaped pincushion. It's great for keeping pins and needles within reach!

PINCUSHION

Recycled item: child-size red sock
You will also need polyester fiberfill, soft-sculpture needle, heavy-duty thread, paper-backed fusible web, green fabric, green felt, hot glue gun, and raffia.

1. Cut cuff from sock; discard cuff.
2. For top of pincushion, leaving a 5" tail of heavy-duty thread at each end, baste along cut edge of sock. Stuff pincushion with fiberfill. Pull thread ends to gather tightly. Knot thread ends together; trim ends.
3. Thread soft-sculpture needle with heavy-duty thread. Leaving a 5" tail of thread at each end and coming up near gathers, insert needle up through bottom of pincushion to top of pincushion. Insert needle $1/8$" away and back through to bottom of pincushion. Pull thread ends to shape pincushion. Knot thread ends together; trim ends.
4. Use pattern, page 151, and follow *Making Appliqués*, page 157, to make leaf appliqué from fabric. Fuse appliqué to felt. Leaving a $1/8$" felt border, cut out leaf. Glue $1/4$" of tip at one end of leaf to top of pincushion.
5. Tie several lengths of raffia into a bow. Glue bow at top of pincushion.

SOCK IT TO ME!

Don't toss those mismatched socks! Cut off the cuffs to fashion these trendy ponytail holders. Simply use elastic thread to sew the raw edges together, adding pony beads as you stitch.

SOCK CUFF PONYTAIL HOLDERS

Recycled items: adult-size socks
You will also need elastic thread and pony beads in assorted colors.

1. For each ponytail holder, cutting through all layers, cut a 2³/₄"w piece from sock cuff. Matching cut edges, fold sock piece in half.
2. Sewing raw edges together, use elastic thread to sew beads along edges of ponytail holder.

COWPOKE'S COMPANION

*R*ustle up a stray sock and a wooden dowel, and your little cowboy will be riding the range in no time! Black felt features, a flowing mane of yarn, and a ribbon bridle transform a stuffed sock into a stately stallion ready for hours of playtime fun.

HOBBY HORSE

Recycled item: adult-size tube sock
You will also need 44" of 1" dia. wooden dowel, hot glue gun, 1"w and 1¹/₂"w grosgrain ribbon, polyester fiberfill, black yarn, tracing paper, red and black felt, assorted black buttons, black embroidery floss, black acrylic paint, paintbrush, and a wooden candle cup with a 1" dia. opening.

Refer to Embroidery Stitches, page 158, before beginning project. Use six strands of floss for all embroidery.

1. Overlapping as necessary to cover dowel and trimming to fit, wrap and glue 1¹/₂"w ribbon around dowel.
2. Stuff sock with fiberfill to within 2" of opening. Insert one end of dowel 4" into sock. Cut a 40" length of yarn. Gather sock around dowel. Gluing ends to secure, wrap yarn tightly around gathers.
3. Trace eye, ear, and mouth patterns, page 145, onto tracing paper; cut out. Using patterns, cut two eyes and two ears from black felt and mouth from red felt.
4. For horse, position and glue eyes on sock near heel. Sew one button to each eye. Position and glue mouth on sock at toe. Work four long *Straight Stitches* across mouth for lips, one *French Knot* on each side of lips, and two large *Cross Stitches* for nostrils. Make a ¹/₄" pleat at

base of each ear; glue to secure. Glue ears to head.
5. For bridle, measure around horse's muzzle; add ¹/₂". Cut a length of 1"w ribbon the determined measurements. Overlapping ends, wrap and glue 1"w ribbon around muzzle. For reins, cut two 45" lengths of 1"w ribbon. Glue one end of each ribbon length to bridle. Glue buttons to sides of bridle.

6. For mane, cut several 11" lengths from yarn. Beginning near ears and gluing one on top of another, glue center of each length to horse.
7. Paint candle cup black; allow to dry. Apply glue to remaining end of dowel. Insert dowel into candle cup.

HUGGABLES' HANGOUT

*Y*our *little one's prized bean bag buddies will love hanging out in this colorful wall caddy! Appliquéd socks are attached to a fabric-covered bulletin board to create the useful unit.*

STUFFED ANIMAL CADDY

Recycled items: framed cork board and adult-size socks

You will also need acrylic paint to coordinate with fabric, paintbrush, batting, fabric, staple gun, hot glue gun, 1/4" dia. decorative cording, paper-backed fusible web, assorted fabrics for appliqués, decorative-edge craft scissors, assorted buttons, upholstery needle, and embroidery floss to coordinate with fabric.

1. Paint wooden frame of cork board; allow to dry.
2. Measure width and length of cork board inside frame. Cut one piece from fabric and two pieces from batting the determined measurements. Layer and staple batting pieces, then fabric to cork board along inside edges of frame.
3. Trimming to fit, glue a length of cording along inside edges of frame, covering staples.
4. Use patterns, page 149, and follow *Making Appliqués*, page 157, to make desired appliqués from fabrics. Trim appliqués with craft scissors as desired. Arrange and fuse appliqués to toe-to-heel areas of socks. Arrange and glue buttons to socks.
5. Roll cuff of each sock down to heel. To attach each sock, thread upholstery needle with embroidery floss. Position sock on cork board. Leaving a 5" tail of floss and working from back of cork board, insert needle through all layers of cork board, heel of sock, then through button. Insert needle back through button, heel of sock, then through all layers of cork board. Tie floss ends at back to secure; trim ends.

MISS "SOCKTOPUS"

Delight a young lady with this cheery jewelry organizer! The helpful "socktopus" is happy to keep a little missy's gems and hair barrettes on hand (or should that be hands!).

SOCKTOPUS

Recycled items: three child-size white tube socks and one adult-size white tube sock

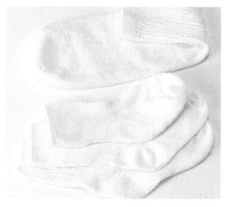

You will also need polyester fiberfill; heavy-duty thread; two $^3/_8$" dia. buttons for eyes; pink, red, and black embroidery floss; yellow yarn; and $^1/_8$"w pink grosgrain ribbon.

Refer to Embroidery Stitches, page 158, before beginning project. Use six strands of floss for all embroidery.

1. Cut eight 3" x 7" pieces from child-size tube socks. For each arm, matching right sides and leaving an opening for turning, sew along cut edges of one sock piece. Turn right side out. Stuff arm with fiberfill; sew opening closed.
2. Arrange arms side by side on a flat surface. Leaving a 5" tail of thread at beginning and end, use heavy-duty thread to sew tops of arms together. Pull thread ends to gather arms into a ring shape.

Knot thread ends together to secure; trim ends.
3. For head, measuring from toe, cut a $4^1/_2$" long piece from toe of adult-size tube sock.
4. Position and sew eyes on head. Use black floss to work *Straight Stitches* for eyelashes. Use pink floss to work *Stem Stitches* for cheeks. Use red floss to work *Straight Stitches* and *Stem Stitches* for mouth.
5. Leaving a 5" tail of thread at beginning and end, use heavy-duty thread to baste along cut edge of head. Pull ends of thread to loosely gather head. Stuff head

with fiberfill. Insert arms in opening at bottom of head. Pull ends of thread to tightly gather bottom of head around arms. Knot thread ends together to secure; trim ends.
6. For each braid, cut fifteen 11" lengths from yarn. Cut two 5" lengths from ribbon. Tie ribbon around yarn lengths 1" from one end. Working with three sets of five strands each, braid yarn lengths together to within 1" of remaining end. Tie remaining ribbon length around yarn lengths. Use a length of yarn to sew braids to top of head.

VESTED INTEREST

*E*ver wish you could salvage a favorite garment that's been ruined by a stubborn stain or a tear? Simply hide those flaws with appliquéd patches made from another worn wearable — a sock! Use fabric scraps to add colorful shapes and borders, and let the loopy texture of the sock's interior give the appliqués added dimension.

SOCK VEST

Recycled items: adult-size white tube socks

You will also need assorted fabrics for appliqués, paper-backed fusible web, desired size vest, and clear nylon thread.

1. Cut one 3" x 6¼" and three 3¼" x 4" pieces each from fabric and web. Fuse web to wrong side of fabric pieces. Arrange and fuse fabric pieces to vest.
2. To prepare each sock, cut sock open along one side, then through toe; flatten sock.
3. Cut one 2" x 5¼" and three 2½" x 3" pieces each from sock pieces and web. Fuse web to right side of sock pieces. Center and fuse sock pieces to fabric pieces on vest.

4. Use patterns, page 141, and follow *Making Appliqués*, page 157, to make one each of small heart, large heart, small star, large star, small leaf, and large leaf appliqués from fabrics. Arrange and fuse appliqués on sock pieces as desired.
5. Follow *Machine Appliqué*, page 157, and use clear nylon thread to stitch around appliqués.

HOMESPUN ACCESSORIES

Add primitive charm to any outfit with these adorable fashion pins. Simply place batting between pieces cut from coffee-dyed socks; then stitch the folksy designs using embroidery floss. Sew on buttons and attach pin backs to complete the homespun jewelry.

SOCK PINS

Recycled items: two adult-size white socks

You will also need instant coffee; drawing compass; tracing paper; batting; tissue paper; straight pins; yellow, dark orange, blue, green, and brown embroidery floss; assorted buttons; hot glue gun; two pin backs; and a ruler.

Refer to Embroidery Stitches, page 158, before beginning project. Use six strands of floss for all embroidery unless otherwise indicated.

CHICKEN PIN

1. Follow *Coffee Dyeing*, page 156, to dye one sock.
2. For pattern, use compass to draw a 3" dia. circle on tracing paper; cut out. Using pattern, cut one piece from batting and two pieces from dyed sock.
3. Trace chicken embroidery pattern, page 152, onto tissue paper. Leaving a 1/2" border around pattern, cut out pattern. Center pattern on one sock piece; pin in place.
4. Referring to pattern, page 152, for floss color, work *Running Stitches* along design lines. Carefully tear away tissue paper.
5. With batting piece between sock pieces, layer and pin batting piece and sock pieces together. Using three strands of

desired color floss and stitching through all layers, work *Backstitches* around design. Cut out pin 1/4" outside stitched line.
6. Use desired color floss to sew buttons to pin. Glue or sew pin back to back of pin.

CAT PIN

1. Follow *Coffee Dyeing*, page 156, to dye remaining sock.
2. For pattern, use ruler to draw a 3" square on tracing paper; cut out. Using pattern, cut one piece from batting and two pieces from sock.
3. Using cat embroidery pattern, page 152, follow Steps 3 and 4 of Chicken Pin to stitch cat design on one sock piece.
4. Using four strands of floss for whiskers, tie a double knot 3/4" from one end of floss. Thread needle with opposite end of floss. Insert needle down through cat's face on sock. Bring needle up 1/4" away. Tie a second double knot in floss next to sock. Clip thread 3/4" from knot.
5. Follow Steps 5 and 6 of Chicken Pin to complete pin.

PETITE PURSE

*P*lease a young lady with this petite purse necklace! It's perfectly precious with buttons and lace, and who would ever know this tiny treasure keeper was made from a worn sock?

SOCK PURSE NECKLACE

Recycled item: child-size sock
You will also need clear nylon thread, decorative trim, pink and green embroidery floss, assorted buttons, fabric, fabric glue, tapestry needle, 28" of ¼"w sheer white ribbon, and a snap.

Refer to Embroidery Stitches, page 158, before beginning project. Use six strands of floss for all embroidery.

1. Measuring from toe of sock, cut a 6" piece from sock. Flatten sock. Beginning at cut edge, cut 2" down each side of sock.
2. For purse flap, cutting through top layer only, cut across sock from cut side to cut side. Use clear nylon thread to blindstitch trim to flap.
3. For flowers on flap, use pink floss to sew three evenly spaced buttons to flap ½" from edge of flap. Use green floss to work *Straight Stitches* for stems and *Lazy Daisies* for leaves.
4. Tear a 1" square from fabric. Glue square to purse; allow to dry. Use pink floss to sew button to center of fabric square.
5. Beginning and ending 3" from ribbon ends and spacing buttons 1½" apart, use tapestry needle to thread buttons onto ribbon. Knot ribbon ends. Tack knots to inside back of purse.
6. Sew one half of snap to inside flap. Sew remaining half of snap to purse.

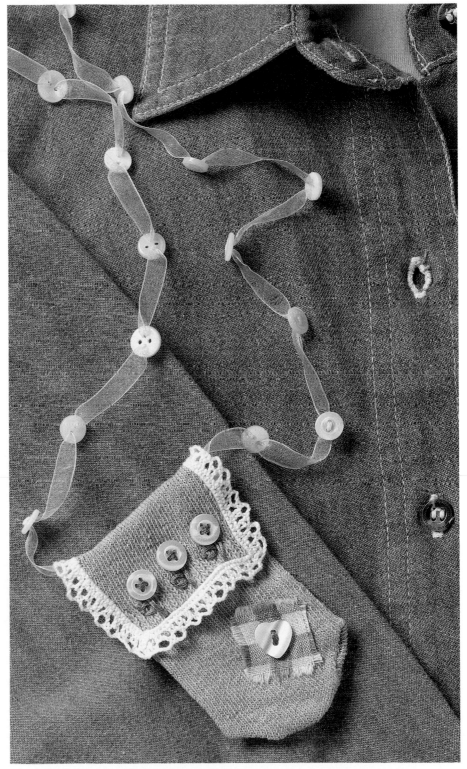

DAINTY TOPPER

*Y*ou can transform an ordinary jar into a lovely gift or storage container using an abandoned sock! Embroider a delicate pattern onto a piece of tea-dyed sock and glue it over half of a foam ball for dimension. A crocheted doily and a ribbon bow make dainty trimmings.

SOCK JAR LID COVER

Recycled item: adult-size white sock

You will also need a tea bag, 6" dia. crocheted doily, drawing compass, tracing paper, transfer paper, green embroidery floss, one-half of a 3" dia. plastic foam ball, low-temperature glue gun, assorted buttons, white and pink pearl beads, ecru spray paint, wide-mouth jar with lid, and 21" of ¼"w ribbon.

Refer to Embroidery Stitches, page 158, before beginning project. Use six strands of floss for all embroidery.

1. Follow *Tea Dyeing*, page 156, to dye sock and doily. Cut sock open along one side, then through toe; flatten sock. Use compass to draw a 7" dia. circle on sock; cut out. Discard remainder of sock.
2. Trace stitching pattern, page 153, onto tracing paper. Use transfer paper to

transfer pattern to center of sock circle. Referring to Stitch Key, page 153, stitch design on sock circle.
3. Center sock circle over rounded side of foam ball half; glue edges of circle to flat side.
4. Spray paint jar lid; allow to dry.

5. Center and glue doily over jar lid. Glue flat side of foam ball half to jar lid. Glue buttons and beads to sock circle as desired.
6. Tie ribbon into a bow around jar lid; spot glue to secure.

WARM AND TOASTY

You'll be amazed at how easy it is to transform an odd sock into a toasty neck warmer! To use, heat the rice-filled warmer in the microwave for two to four minutes or just until warm. What a great gift for anyone who suffers from neck pain!

SOCK NECK WARMER

Recycled item: adult-size knee sock

You will also need two 12" lengths of $1^{1}/_{2}$"w grosgrain ribbon and whole grain rice.

1. Measuring from cuff and cutting through all layers, cut a $21^{1}/_{2}$" long tube from sock.
2. Fold one end of tube $^{1}/_{4}$" to inside. Place one ribbon length between folds at center; sew to secure.
3. Fill sock with rice to within $2^{1}/_{4}$" of remaining end.
4. Repeat Step 2 to finish opposite end.

SNOW FOLK FOR ALL SEASONS

*O*ur frosty friends are a cinch to make — and you can fashion one for every season of the year! Create the simple snow people by stuffing socks with fiberfill; then dress them up for winter, spring, summer, and fall.

FOUR SEASONS SNOW FOLK

Refer to Embroidery Stitches, page 158, before beginning project.

BASIC SNOW BODY
Recycled items: adult-size white socks
You will also need polyester fiberfill, white and black embroidery floss, hot glue gun, two ⁵⁄₁₆" dia. black buttons, utility scissors, toothpick, and an orange permanent medium-point marker.

1. For body, cut cuff from one sock; discard cuff. Leaving a 5" tail of thread at beginning and end, baste along cut edge of body. Stuff body with fiberfill. Pull thread ends to gather tightly. Knot thread ends together; trim ends. For neck, tie a length of white floss around body.
2. Glue buttons to head for eyes. Use utility scissors to cut a 1¼" long piece from toothpick for nose. Use marker to "paint" nose. Apply glue to cut end of nose. Work cut end of nose into head. Use six strands of black floss to work one long *Straight Stitch* for mouth. Use six strands of black floss to work one *French Knot* on each side of mouth.

SPRING SNOW WOMAN

Recycled items: twigs

You will also need garden clippers, hot glue gun, Basic Snow Body, 4" dia. artificial flower with leaves, three $1/4$" dia. black buttons, $3/4$" dia. artificial flowers in assorted colors, 2"h basket, and a 4" dia. grapevine wreath.

1. Use garden clippers to cut two 4" twigs. Glue one twig to each side of snow body for arms.
2. For hat, glue center of 4" dia. flower to head.
3. Glue buttons to front of snow body.
4. Glue $3/4$" dia. flowers in basket. Glue basket to one arm.
5. For base, arrange and glue $3/4$" dia. flowers on wreath.
6. Glue bottom of snow body to base.

SUMMER SNOW WOMAN

Recycled items: adult-size pink sock, twigs, and an adult-size blue sock

You will also need a Basic Snow Body, garden clippers, hot glue gun, wire cutters, $1 1/2$"w sunglasses pin, 6" dia. crocheted hat including brim, one $1/4$" dia. black button, 4" dia. grapevine wreath, and 21" of $1/4$" dia. white cord.

1. Measuring from finished edge of cuff and cutting through all layers, cut one $1 1/4$"w piece and one $2 1/4$"w piece from cuff of pink sock.
2. For bikini top, fold each cut edge of $1 1/4$"w cuff piece $1/4$" to wrong side. For front of bikini top, work a *Running Stitch* from fold to fold in top; do not trim thread ends. Pull thread ends to gather top tightly; knot thread ends to secure. Place top on snow body 1" below neck.

3. For bikini bottom, fold each cut edge of $2 1/4$"w cuff piece $1/4$" to wrong side. Place bottom on snow body $1 1/4$" below bikini top.
4. Use garden clippers to cut two 3" twigs. Glue one twig to each side of snow body for arms.
5. Use wire cutters to remove pin back from sunglasses pin. Glue sunglasses over eyes. Glue hat to head. Glue button to front of snow body.
6. For base, cut a piece from blue sock large enough to cover wreath. Wrap sock piece around wreath; whipstitch edges together. Knot ends of cord together 1" from end. Arrange and glue cord around base.
7. Glue bottom of snow body to base.

FALL SNOWMAN

Recycled items: twigs

You will also need garden clippers, hot glue gun, Basic Snow Body, artificial leaves, 4" dia. straw hat including brim, miniature rake, two $1/4$" dia. black buttons, and a 4" dia. grapevine wreath.

1. Use garden clippers to cut two $3 1/2$" twigs. Glue one twig to each side of snow body for arms.
2. Glue one leaf to hat and one to rake. Glue hat to head. Glue rake to arms; spot glue across body to secure. Glue buttons to front of snow body.
3. For base, arrange and glue leaves around wreath.
4. Glue bottom of snow body to base.

WINTER SNOWMAN

Recycled items: adult-size red sock, twigs, and a red-and-green striped toddler-size sock

You will also need a Basic Snow Body, garden clippers, hot glue gun, three $1/4$" dia. black buttons, batting, 4" dia. grapevine wreath, and an artificial evergreen garland with red berries.

1. Measuring from finished edge of cuff and cutting through all layers, cut one $4 1/2$"w piece from cuff of red sock.
2. With finished edge at neck, place sock piece on snow body for shirt. Fold finished edge $3/4$" to right side twice.
3. Use garden clippers to cut two 3" twigs. Glue one twig to each side of snow body for arms.
4. For hat, measuring from finished edge of cuff and cutting through all layers, cut a $3 3/4$"w piece from striped sock. Turn sock piece wrong side out. Gather cut edge and glue to secure; turn right side out. Fold finished edge $1 1/4$" to right side twice. Place hat on head; spot glue to secure.
5. Glue buttons to front of snow body.
6. For base, cut a piece of batting large enough to cover wreath. Wrap batting piece around wreath; glue edges to secure. Trimming to fit, glue garland around wreath.
7. Glue bottom of snow body to base.

ALL
BOXED UP

Shake up those boring brown boxes with some bold new ideas! Whether you need a cozy bed for Kitty or a wastebasket for the bedroom, we have a bounty of original ways to reclaim those cardboard containers. Besides the many attractive organizers you can create, there are wonderful playtime projects to inspire a frontier soldier or to please a proud little princess. For grown-ups, make a darling desk set for her and a masculine clutter-catcher for him. Then sit back and prop your feet on a comfy vegetable crate ottoman or check out the time on your clever "new" clock. Congratulate yourself — you're thinking outside the box!

97

Packed with flower power, this space-saving storage unit is constructed from three cardboard boxes. Simply stack and glue the boxes, cover with fabric, and add floral appliqués. What a great addition to a little girl's room!

STACKED BOX ORGANIZER

Recycled items: three large cardboard boxes of equal width (we used one $6^1/2$" x $9^1/2$" x $9^3/4$" box and two $8^1/2$" x $9^1/2$" x $9^3/4$" boxes)

You will also need a craft knife, cutting mat, hot glue gun, assorted fabrics, spray adhesive, batting, foam core board, paper backed fusible web, and pink glitter dimensional paint.

Refer to Painting Techniques, page 156, before beginning project.

1. To prepare each box, use craft knife to cut top from box, if necessary.
2. With open sides facing front, stack and glue boxes together.
3. Including top and bottom, measure around sides of stack; add 1". Measure depth of stack at deepest area; add 4". Cut a piece from fabric the determined measurements, piecing as necessary. Apply spray adhesive to outside of stack. Overlapping short ends at bottom of stack, center and smooth fabric piece around stack. Smooth excess fabric onto back of stack; spot glue if necessary. Clipping as necessary, smooth excess fabric at front of stack to inside of each box.
4. Measure depth of each box. Measure around inside of each box. Cut a piece from fabric for each box the determined measurements. Apply spray adhesive to inside of each box. Smooth each fabric piece to insides of boxes.
5. Measure width and length of back of stack. Cut a piece from fabric the determined measurements. Apply spray adhesive to back of stack; smooth onto stack.

6. Measure width of boxes; cut two strips from fabric 4" by the determined measurement. Apply spray adhesive to wrong side of each strip. Centering strip over front edge of shelf, smooth strips onto top and onto underside of both inner shelves.
7. Measure width and length of inside bottom of each box. Cut a piece from batting the determined measurements. Use craft knife to cut a piece of foam core board the determined measurements. Cut one piece of fabric 2" larger on all sides than foam core board piece. Place fabric wrong side up on flat surface. Center batting, then foam core board piece on fabric. Fold corners of fabric diagonally over corners of foam core board; glue to secure. Fold edges of fabric over edges of foam core board; glue to secure.
8. Use patterns, page 144, and follow *Making Appliqués*, page 157, to make six each of small flower and small center appliqués and seven each of large flower and large center appliqués. Arrange and fuse one large flower and one large center on each fabric-covered foam core board piece. Arrange and fuse remaining appliqués to sides of organizer. Use dimensional paint to outline petals and centers of each flower; allow to dry. Glue fabric-covered foam core board pieces inside back of boxes.

Children will have hours of fun at this awesome activity center! Choose two coordinating fabrics to create a cover for the box and add pockets and bands for holding toys. It's a great way to beat the rainy day blues and recycle, too!

ACTIVITY CENTER BOX

Recycled item: cardboard box at least 14"h x 17"w (our box measures 15¼" x 17⅛" x 17¾")

You will also need two coordinating fabrics, 1"w paper-backed fusible web tape, straight pins, ¾"w elastic, and a safety pin.

Match right sides and use a ⅝" seam allowance for all sewing.

1. Measure width and length of top of box; add 1¼" to each measurement. Cut one piece from first fabric the determined measurements.

2. Measure height of box; add 2⅝". Measure width of each side of box; add 1¼" to each width measurement. Cut a piece from first fabric for each side the determined measurements.

3. For cover, sew side pieces together, end to end, to form a tube. Matching wrong sides and corners of top fabric piece with seams of tube, and pivoting as necessary, sew top fabric piece to sides.

4. Trimming to fit, fuse a length of web tape along bottom edges of cover; do not remove paper backing. Press edges 1" to wrong side. Remove paper backing and fuse to secure. Turn cover right side out.

5. For each pocket, cut a 15" x 24¼" piece from second fabric. Trimming to fit, fuse a length of web tape along one long edge; do not remove paper backing. Press edge 1" to wrong side. Remove paper backing and fuse to secure. Press sides and remaining long edge (bottom) of pocket ⅝" to wrong side.

6. Press one ¾"w pleat ¼" from each side at bottom of pocket and two 1"w pleats ⅛" apart at center bottom of pocket (Fig. 1). Pin to secure.

Fig. 1

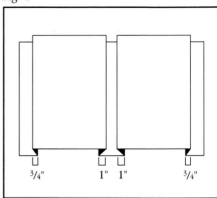

7. Pin pocket to one side piece 2" from bottom. Sew along each side and across bottom of pocket, being careful to not catch pleat in stitching. Sew vertically through center of pocket between pleats.

8. Cut four 15¼" lengths of elastic and four 2¼" x 25¼" strips from second fabric. For each elastic strip, press short ends of one fabric strip ⅝" to wrong side. Matching wrong sides, sew along long edges of fabric strip to form tube. Turn tube right side out. Gathering fabric to fit, use safety pin to thread elastic through tube; catching elastic in stitches, sew across ends to secure.

9. Spacing elastic strips 5" apart, center and pin two strips 4" from bottom to each remaining side. Sewing through all layers, sew across each end of each elastic strip, then at 3½" to 4" intervals.

10. Place cover over box.

BABY-SOFT FRAME

*I*deal *for that darling snapshot of baby, our chenille-covered frame is easy to fashion from a cardboard gift box. For unique accents, tie infant socks together with chenille stems to create magical butterflies. It's a great shower gift for an expectant mom!*

CHENILLE-COVERED BOX FRAME

Recycled item: 5" x 7" or larger cardboard gift box with lid

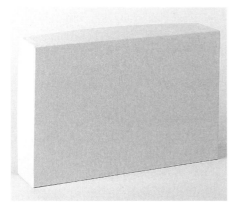

You will also need a craft knife, cutting mat, chenille fabric, ruler, spray adhesive, photograph to fit in mat, 4" x 6" purchased mat with a $3^1/_2$" x 5" opening, hot glue gun, three pairs of infant-size socks, white bump chenille stem, assorted color chenille stems, $^1/_8$" dia. pom-poms, assorted buttons, fabric to coordinate with chenille fabric, cardboard, and 4" of $^5/_8$"w satin ribbon.

1. For frame, remove lid from box. Use craft knife to cut a $3^1/_2$" x $5^1/_2$" opening in center of lid. Follow *Covering a Box*, page 159, to cover lid with chenille fabric. Cutting to within $^1/_8$" of each corner of opening in lid, use craft knife to cut an "X" in fabric. Smooth fabric to inside of lid. Mount photograph in mat. Glue mat inside opening.

2. For each butterfly, fold cuffs of one pair of socks 1" to inside. Arrange socks to form an "X." Cut one bump from bump chenille stem; wrap around socks at center to secure.

3. For antennae, cut $3^1/_2$" from one chenille stem; discard remaining portion of stem. Thread chenille stem piece under bump chenille on butterfly; curl ends. Glue pom-poms to butterflies. Arrange and glue butterflies and buttons on frame.

4. Follow *Covering a Box* to cover box with coordinating fabric.

5. Place frame on box; glue to secure.

6. For frame stand, measure height of back of box. Cut a piece from cardboard 2"w by the determined measurement. Bend one end of stand $1^1/_4$" to one side. Cut a piece from coordinating fabric large enough to cover all sides of stand. Apply spray adhesive to wrong side of fabric piece. Wrap fabric around stand. Glue short section of frame stand 1" below center top of back of box. Glue one end of ribbon to back of box; glue remaining end to frame stand (Fig. 1).

Fig. 1

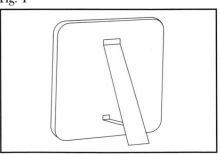

DRESS-UP TIME

*L*ittle ladies will love storing their dress-up trinkets and treasures in this Victorian-inspired trunk! Crumpled tissue paper and vintage motifs are decoupaged on a cardboard box and lid to create the quaint chest.

DRESS-UP CHEST

Recycled item: large cardboard box with lid (we used a 10$\frac{1}{2}$" x 11$\frac{1}{4}$" x 17$\frac{1}{2}$" box) *You will also need* white spray primer; several sheets of white tissue paper to cover box and lid; foam brush; decoupage glue; pink, purple, and green acrylic paint; household sponges; Victorian-motif wrapping paper; gold paint pen; 5" dia. gold paper doily; clear acrylic spray sealer; household cement; and items to decorate chest (we used assorted acrylic jewels and charms).

Refer to Painting Techniques, page 156, before beginning project. Allow primer, paint, sealer, and household cement to dry after each application.

1. Apply primer to lid and box.
2. Lightly crumple tissue paper; smooth out. Trimming to fit and overlapping as necessary, cut enough pieces from tissue paper to cover lid and box. Use foam brush to apply decoupage glue to outside of lid and box. Overlapping edges as necessary, smooth tissue paper onto lid and box. Fold excess tissue paper to inside of lid and box; spot glue and allow to dry.
3. Sponge paint lid and box green. Lightly sponge paint lid and box pink, then purple.

4. Cut desired motifs from wrapping paper. Use foam brush to apply decoupage glue to backs of motifs. Arrange and smooth motifs onto lid and box; allow to dry. Use pen to outline motifs and add details to lid and box.
5. Cut doily in half. Use foam brush to apply decoupage glue to backs of doily pieces. Smooth doily pieces onto bottom front corners of box; allow to dry.
6. Apply two to three coats of sealer to lid and box.
7. Arrange decorative items on lid and box; use household cement to glue in place.

PICTURE THIS!

*D*on't let those precious photos *sit unnoticed in a box or album! Display them on this easy brag board made from cardboard, batting, and fabric. Tuck your favorite snapshots under the ribbon latticework and enjoy the heartwarming results of your simple labor of love!*

PHOTO SCREEN

Recycled item: cardboard box

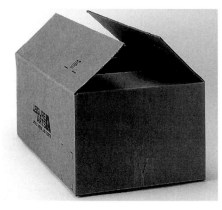

You will also need a craft knife, cutting mat, fabric, batting, hot glue gun, and $^3/_8$"w grosgrain ribbon.

1. Use craft knife to cut three $8^1/_2$" x $20^1/_2$" pieces from cardboard box for panels; discard remainder of box.
2. For each panel, cut one $9^1/_2$" x $21^1/_2$" piece and one 9" x 21" piece from fabric and two $8^1/_2$" x $20^1/_2$" pieces from batting. Glue one piece of batting to each side of panel. For front, center and glue $9^1/_2$" x $21^1/_2$" fabric piece on one side of panel. Fold and glue fabric edges to back of panel.
3. For holding straps, cut six 14" lengths from ribbon. Wrapping ends of ribbon to back of panel, arrange and glue ribbon lengths on panel to form a grid.

4. For photo screen, arrange panels, front side down, side by side on a flat surface. Cut ten 4" lengths from ribbon. For hinges, spacing evenly, glue one end of five ribbon lengths to each long edge of center panel. Glue opposite ribbon ends to side panels.
5. Press edges of each 9" x 21" fabric piece $^1/_4$" to wrong side. Center and glue one fabric piece to back of each panel.

TIMELY BEAUTY

*K*eeping time has never brought this much beauty to your home! Our delicate Victorian-style clock is crafted from an empty box and features a face made from an old greeting card. Embellish the timepiece with wired ribbon and a silk flower to complete the feminine look.

BOX CLOCK

Recycled items: cardboard box (we used a 1³/₈" x 5¹/₂" x 7" box) and a greeting card to fit on box

You will also need fabric, ruler, spray adhesive, craft knife, cutting mat, hot glue gun, push pin, quartz battery operated clock movement for a ¹/₄" thick clock face, 35" of 1¹/₂"w wired ribbon, and a 2" dia. artificial flower.

1. Follow *Covering a Box*, page 159, to cover box with fabric.
2. Cut card front from card; discard card back. Center and glue card front to box.
3. For clock, use push pin to make a pilot hole through center of card and box. Working from back, insert shaft of clock movement through pilot hole. Follow manufacturer's instructions to attach hands to clock movement.

4. Tie ribbon into a bow; notch ends. With streamers at back of clock, glue knot of bow to top of clock. Arrange and glue streamers to back of clock. Glue flower to knot of bow.

Youthful fancies will take flight when presented with this mighty play fortress! Cardboard boxes covered with paper-bag "stones" give this structure its rugged appearance. Youngsters will have hours of fun defending their stronghold against imaginary foes!

PLAY FORT

Recycled items: two large boxes and large brown paper bags

You will also need a craft knife, cutting mat, hot glue gun, hammer, nail, $1^{7}/_{8}$" of $^{5}/_{16}$" dia. wooden dowel, three 1" dia. wooden beads, corrugated craft cardboard, paintbrush, brown acrylic paint, and grey spray primer.

Use craft knife for all cutting unless otherwise indicated.

1. For each box, unfold flaps at top and bottom of box.
2. Beginning at edge of bottom box flap on one side of one box, cut up, across, then down to cut a large rectangle in center of one side of box the desired size for doorway between boxes. Repeat to cut the same size rectangle in one side of

remaining box. Set aside cardboard cut from boxes. Matching doorway openings, glue boxes together.
3. Cut four 5" x $6^{1}/_{2}$" strips from cardboard remnants for each box. Fold each strip in half to score. For stability, glue strips inside boxes at corners of bottom box flaps only of each box.
4. Cut desired windows in boxes. Set aside cardboard cut from boxes.
5. For trim on each window, measure window from top to bottom. Cut two strips from cardboard remnants $1^{1}/_{2}$"w by the determined measurement. Glue one strip along each side of window. Measure across window; add 3". Cut two strips from cardboard remnants $1^{1}/_{2}$"w by the determined measurement. Center and glue strips along top and bottom of window.
6. Beginning at edge of bottom box flap several inches from one corner of one box, cut up, then across to cut a desired size door in front of box. Beginning several inches down from top of door, cut down, across, then up to cut a window flap in door.
7. For door handle, use hammer and nail to punch a hole in door at desired position. Thread dowel through hole. Glue one bead to each end of dowel. Glue remaining bead to back of window flap.
8. For trim on door, measure door from top to bottom. Cut two strips from cardboard remnants $1^{1}/_{2}$"w by the determined measurement. Glue one strip along each side of door. Measure across door; add 3". Cut one strip from cardboard remnants $1^{1}/_{2}$"w by the determined measurement. Center and glue strip along top of door.
9. For flat roof, glue top flaps of one box closed. Measure width and length of box

top. Cut a piece from corrugated cardboard the determined measurements. Glue cardboard piece to box top.
10. For roof peaks, marking at top edge of box on front of remaining box, mark center of box. Lightly draw a line across front of box 10" below top edge of box. Cutting at an angle, cut from mark at center top of box to each side of box at drawn line. Repeat to cut peak from back of box.
11. For roof, measure from one side edge of one peak to top of peak, then to opposite side edge of peak. Measure from top of front peak to top of back peak. Cut a piece from cardboard the determined measurements. Fold cardboard piece in half to score; unfold. Position and glue roof to roof peaks.
12. For shingles, cut enough 4" x 7" pieces from cardboard remnants to cover roof. Layer and glue shingles to roof. For top shingles, fold several shingles in half to score. Layer and glue scored shingles to top of roof.
13. Use a dry paintbrush to paint window and door trim, door, top of flat roof and shingles brown; allow to dry.
14. To prepare each bag, cut bag open along one fold; cut away and discard bottom of bag. Press bag with a warm, dry iron.
15. Lightly spray unprinted sides of each bag with primer; allow to dry. Tear bags into squares of assorted sizes. For rocks, shape squares around fist. Arrange and glue rocks to fort.

TAKE NOTE!

*B*e sure to "take note" of this decorative project . . . it'll really help you get things organized! A piece cut from a cardboard box provides the back for the holder, and lengths of wide ribbon are glued on to create pockets. Choose both solid and print ribbons to make your card holder unique!

NOTE CARD HOLDER

Recycled items: cardboard box at least 16" x 18" and a large brown paper bag

You will also need a craft knife; cutting mat; 1⅝"w, 3½"w, and 3⅝"w coordinating ribbons; hot glue gun; assorted 1⅛" dia. cream buttons; and 8" of medium-gauge craft wire.

1. Use craft knife to cut one 15" x 17¾" cardboard piece from box; discard remainder of box.
2. For pockets, cut two 17" lengths each of 1⅝"w and 3½"w ribbons and three 17" lengths of 3⅝"w ribbon.
3. For top edge of holder, position one 3⅝"w ribbon along one short end of cardboard piece with one long edge of ribbon extending ½" and each end of ribbon extending 1" beyond edges of cardboard piece. Glue bottom edge of ribbon to front of cardboard piece. Glue ends of ribbon to back of cardboard piece.
4. Position one 1⅝"w ribbon on front of cardboard piece with one long edge overlapping bottom edge of previous ribbon and each short end of ribbon extending 1" beyond edge of cardboard piece. Glue bottom edge of ribbon to front of cardboard piece. Glue ends of ribbon to back of cardboard piece. Repeat to layer and glue remaining 1⅝"w ribbon, 3½"w ribbons, and one 3⅝"w ribbon to cardboard piece.
5. Position remaining 3⅝"w ribbon along remaining end of cardboard piece with bottom edge of ribbon extending ½" and each end of ribbon extending 1" beyond edges of cardboard piece. Glue bottom edge, then short ends of ribbon to back of cardboard piece.
6. Glue buttons to corners of card holder.
7. Cut a 14½" x 17¼" piece from paper bag; center and glue on back of card holder.
8. For hanger, crimp 1" of each end of wire; glue ends to back of card holder.

COMPUTER "SCREEN SAVER"

*P*ersonalize your workstation with our "screen saver!" This inventive message center makes great use of space that you view every day. Simply apply cork to a frame cut from a cardboard box; then trim with jute twine. Cut pretty motifs from greeting cards to dress up ordinary thumbtacks.

COMPUTER CORKBOARD

Recycled items: large cardboard box and greeting cards

You will also need tracing paper, removable tape, craft knife, cutting mat, foam brush, craft glue, craft cork sheeting, hot glue gun, jute twine, thumbtacks, and double-sided mounting tape.

Allow craft glue to dry after each application. Use hot glue for all gluing unless otherwise indicated.

1. Carefully disassemble box; lay flat.
2. For frame pattern, draw around outside edge of screen on tracing paper; cut out. Leaving at least 2" of cardboard on all sides, tape pattern on flattened box. Use craft knife to cut out frame 2" larger on all sides than pattern. Cut frame opening along pattern edges; remove pattern.
3. Use foam brush to apply craft glue to frame. Press cork sheeting onto frame. Use craft knife to trim cork sheeting even with edges of frame.
4. Trimming to fit, glue a length of twine around inside edge of frame. Leaving a 4" tail at each end and beginning and ending at center bottom, glue a length of twine around outside edge of frame. Knot ends of twine together.
5. Cut desired motifs from cards. Glue one motif to frame above knot. For decorative thumbtacks, glue motifs to heads of thumbtacks.
6. Use tape to attach corkboard to monitor.

DREAMY HEADBOARD

FABRIC-COVERED HEADBOARD

Add a soft touch to a guest room with this feminine headboard! Made from a cardboard box and fabric bolt rolls, the headboard's dreamy appearance is enhanced by checked and patchwork-print fabrics.

Recycled items: 36" x 45" cardboard box and three 2¹/₂" dia. x 54" long fabric bolt cylinders

You will also need a craft knife, cutting mat, assorted fabrics, batting, staple gun, hot glue gun, white acrylic paint, paintbrush, two 3¹/₄" dia. papier-mâché balls, and ¹/₄" dia. white cord.

1. Unfold flaps at top and bottom of box. Use craft knife to cut along one corner of box; flatten box. Cut a 35" x 43¹/₂" piece from box. Discard remainder of box.
2. Measure height and width of cardboard piece. Cut one piece from fabric and two pieces from batting the determined measurements, piecing as necessary. Staple one batting piece to each side of cardboard piece. For back of headboard, staple fabric piece to one side of cardboard piece.
3. For front of headboard, measure height and width of cardboard piece; add 4" to each measurement. Cut a piece from fabric the determined measurements, piecing as necessary. Press each edge ¹/₄" to wrong side. Center fabric on remaining side of cardboard piece. Fold fabric to back of headboard; staple to secure.
4. For top railing, measure width of headboard. Cut a length from one fabric bolt the determined measurement. Cut a 10¹/₂"w piece from batting by the determined measurement. Wrap batting around top railing; staple to secure. Measure length of top railing; add 2". Measure around top railing; add 1". Cut a piece from fabric the determined measurements. Overlapping edges at back and to inside of railing as necessary, wrap and glue fabric piece around railing. Glue railing to top of headboard.
5. For each side post, measure height of headboard; add 7¹/₂". Cut one length from one remaining fabric bolt the determined measurement. Cut a 10¹/₂"w piece from batting by the determined measurement. Wrap batting around side post; staple to secure. Measure length of side post; add 2". Measure around side post; add 1". Cut a piece from fabric the determined measurements. Overlapping edges at back and to inside of side post as necessary, wrap and glue fabric piece around post. Glue one post to each side of headboard.
6. Paint each papier-mâché ball; allow to dry. For each ball, cut two ⁵/₈" x 13" strips from fabric. Crossing at top of ball, arrange and glue strips on ball. Glue one ball to top of each side post.
7. Trimming to fit, glue a length of cord to headboard below top railing. Trimming to fit, glue a length of cord to headboard along each side post from bottom of headboard over top railing.

Little things mean a lot, and nobody knows that better than a collector of miniatures! This petite but sturdy display shelf is finished with dollhouse trims for structural interest. Who would ever guess that it began as three processed cheese food boxes?

CARDBOARD BOX CURIO SHELF

Recycled items: three 2⅝" x 3" x 9" cardboard boxes and a large brown paper bag

You will also need white spray paint, ½"w decorative doll house molding, ⅝"w decorative doll house trim, hot glue gun, fabric, spray adhesive, and a craft saw.

1. Spray paint inside of each box, molding, and decorative trim white; allow to dry.
2. For shelf, stack and glue boxes side by side.
3. Measure around outside of shelf; add 1". Measure depth of shelf. Cut a piece from fabric the determined measurements. Apply spray adhesive to wrong side of fabric piece. Overlapping ends at bottom of shelf, smooth fabric piece around outside of shelf.
4. Draw around outside edge of shelf on paper bag; cut out ⅛" inside drawn line. Apply spray adhesive to wrong side of bag piece. Smooth bag piece on back of shelf.
5. Measure width of one inner shelf. Use saw to cut two pieces of decorative trim the determined measurement. Glue trim to inner shelves.
6. For top and bottom molding pieces, measure width of top of shelf. Use saw to cut two pieces of molding the determined measurement. For side molding pieces, measure height of shelf; subtract ½". Use saw to cut two pieces of molding the determined measurement. Arrange and glue top, bottom, then side molding pieces to shelf.

TREASURE CHEST

Here's a pretty storage chest for special treasures — and no one will believe it began as a salt container and an ordinary box! Cover the boxes with batting and fabric; then add intricate lace and trims to give it a feminine feel.

PADDED STORAGE CHEST

Recycled items: 3¹/₂" dia. x 5¹/₂"h salt container and a 1³/₈" x 3¹/₂" x 5¹/₂" cardboard box

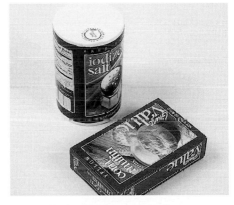

You will also need a craft knife, cutting mat, hot glue gun, batting, pinking shears, fabric, ¹/₄"w gimp trim, pregathered lace, and 7" of ¹/₄"w satin ribbon.

1. For lid, use craft knife to cut salt container in half lengthwise; discard one half.
2. For bottom of chest, use glue to reseal box. Use craft knife to cut along one long edge and two short edges of box front. For hinge, trim box front to 1" (Fig. 1). Glue hinge inside lid.

Fig. 1

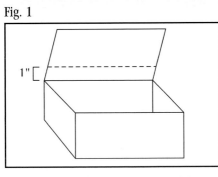

3. Trimming to fit, cut one piece of batting large enough to cover lid and chest. Glue batting to outside of lid and chest.

4. Use pinking shears to cut enough 2" squares from fabric to cover lid and bottom of chest. Overlapping as necessary to cover chest, glue fabric squares to outside of lid and chest.
5. Cut two 7" lengths of gimp trim. Glue one length over top of lid ¹/₂" from each side.
6. Measure around opening edge and back of lid; add ¹/₂". Cut one length each of lace and gimp trim the determined measurement. Overlapping ends at back, glue lace, then trim around lid. Tie ribbon into a bow. Glue bow to center front of lid.

*S*till looking for the perfect accent to fill that empty corner? Create this attractive table using an ordinary cardboard box! You choose the fabrics to match your decor and fashion the skirt without a single stitch. Tack on a tassel to give the table a classy touch.

COVERED BOX TABLE

Recycled item: large cardboard box (our box measures 18½" x 24" x 24¾")

You will also need two coordinating fabrics, spray adhesive, 1"w fusible web tape, and a tassel.

1. Measure height of box. Cut four strips from first fabric 6"w by the determined measurement. Apply spray adhesive to wrong side of each fabric strip. Overlapping 3" onto sides of box, center and smooth one fabric strip to each corner of box.
2. For side table skirt, measure from bottom of one side edge, over top, to bottom of opposite side edge of box; add 4". Measure width of side of box; add 4". Cut one piece from second fabric the determined measurements. Trimming to fit, fuse a length of web tape along each

edge; do not remove paper backing. Press each edge 2" to wrong side. Remove paper backing and fuse short ends, then long edges to secure. Center and place fabric piece on box from side to side.
3. For front and back table skirt, measure from bottom front edge of box, over top, to bottom back edge of box; add 4". Measure width of top of box; add 4". Cut one piece from second fabric the determined measurements. Trimming to fit, fuse a length of web tape to each edge; do not remove paper backing. Press each edge 2" to wrong side. Remove paper backing and fuse short ends, then long edges to secure. Center and place fabric piece on box from front to back.
4. For side table topper, measure top of box from side to side; add 24". Measure top of box from front to back; add 4". Cut a piece from first fabric the determined measurements. Matching long edges, fold table topper in half. Refer to Fig. 1 to cut a point at each short end of table topper.

Fig. 1

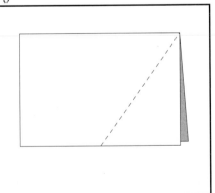

5. Trimming to fit, fuse a length of web tape to wrong side of topper along each long edge; do not remove paper backing. Press each edge 2" to wrong side. Remove paper backing and fuse in place. For each end, trimming to fit, fuse a length of web tape to wrong side of topper along edge of one side of point; do not remove paper backing. Press 2" to wrong side. Remove paper backing and fuse in place. Repeat to fuse remaining side of point.
6. Center and place fabric piece on box from side to side.
7. For front table topper, measure top of box from front to back; add 24". Measure top of box from side to side; add 4". Cut a piece from first fabric the determined measurements. Matching short edges, fold table topper in half. Refer to Fig. 1 to cut a point at each long end of table topper.
8. Repeat Step 5 to finish edges of table topper.
9. Center and place fabric piece on box from front to back. Tack tassel to front of table topper.

DARLING DOLL DECOR

Any little girl knows that even dolls and bean-bag pals need a comfy place to sleep! A darling addition to the playhouse, our cigar box doll bed features thread-spool legs, doll pin bedposts, and a soft, cushy mattress. She'll love the pretty patchwork quilt and bolster pillow, too.

DOLL BED

Recycled item: $2^{1}/_{2}$" x $5^{1}/_{2}$" x $8^{1}/_{2}$" cigar box

You will also need a craft knife; cutting mat; wrapping paper; spray adhesive; ruler; hot glue gun; pink acrylic paint; paintbrush; two wooden doll pins; two $^{1}/_{2}$" dia. white plastic beads; assorted fabrics for feet, mattress, quilt top, and pillow; four wooden spools of equal size; polyester fiberfill; batting; chenille needle; yarn; and two 9" lengths of $^{1}/_{8}$"w ribbon.

Match right sides and raw edges and use a $^{1}/_{4}$" seam allowance for all sewing.

1. Use craft knife to cut lid from box. Cut a 5" x $5^{1}/_{2}$" piece from lid for headboard. Cut a piece from wrapping paper large enough to cover all sides of headboard. Apply spray adhesive to wrong side of paper. Wrap paper around headboard.
2. Follow *Covering a Box*, page 159, to cover box with wrapping paper. For bed, glue headboard to one short end of box.
3. Paint doll pins pink; allow to dry. Glue beads to top of doll pins. Glue one doll pin on each side of headboard.

4. Trimming to fit, glue fabric around each spool. Glue one spool to each corner of bottom of bed for legs.
5. For mattress, cut two $6^{3}/_{4}$" x $10^{1}/_{4}$" pieces from fabric. Leaving an opening for turning, sew pieces together. Turn right side out. Stuff mattress with fiberfill; sew opening closed. Place mattress on bed.
6. For quilt top, cut fifty-six $1^{1}/_{2}$" squares from fabrics. Sew seven squares into a row; repeat to make a total of eight rows. Matching seams, sew rows together along long edges; press.
7. Cut one 9" x 10" piece each from batting and fabric. Place quilt top right side up on a flat surface. Layer fabric, then batting on quilt top. Sewing through all layers and leaving an opening for turning, sew quilt together. Clip corners; turn right side out. Sew opening closed. Use chenille needle to thread 4" lengths of yarn through quilt as desired. Knot yarn ends at top of quilt; trim ends.
8. For pillow, cut one 6" x $6^{1}/_{2}$" piece from fabric. Cut two 2" x 6" strips from a second fabric. Press long edges of each strip $^{1}/_{4}$" to wrong side. Matching wrong sides and pressed edges, press fabric strips in half. Insert one short edge of 6" x $6^{1}/_{2}$" fabric piece in fold of one strip; sew along edges of fabric strip to secure. Repeat with opposite short edge and fabric strip. Sew pillow together along long edges. Turn right side out. Gather one end of pillow at fabric strip. Tie one length of ribbon around pillow at gathers. Stuff middle of pillow with fiberfill. Gather opposite end of pillow at fabric strip. Tie remaining length of ribbon around opposite end of pillow at gathers.

BEAN BAG BLAST

*L*ooking for a fun and inexpensive children's party game or rainy day activity? Well, look no further! This bright bean bag toss is easy to make using fabric-covered cardboard boxes and self-adhesive numbers. The bags stitch up in a jiffy, too!

BAG TOSS GAME

Recycled item: one $16^{1}/_{2}$" x $20^{3}/_{4}$" x 27" cardboard box

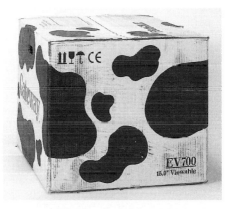

You will also need a craft knife, cutting mat, heavyweight cardboard, hot glue gun, drawing compass, assorted fabrics, spray adhesive, tracing paper, self-adhesive felt numbers, $1^{3}/_{4}$" dia. wooden ball knob, and dried beans.

1. Unfold flaps at top and bottom of box. Use craft knife to cut top flaps from box. Use craft knife to cut two $4^{1}/_{2}$" x 6" strips from cardboard. Fold each strip in half to score. For stability, glue strips across corners of front bottom box flaps only.
2. For openings, use compass to draw three $4^{1}/_{2}$" dia. circles on front of box. Use craft knife to cut out circles.
3. Measure height and width of front of box; add 2" to each measurement. Cut two pieces from fabric the determined measurements. Apply spray adhesive to wrong side of each fabric piece. Overlapping onto sides and inside of box as necessary, center and smooth one fabric piece to front of box and one fabric piece to back of box. Use craft knife to cut an "X" in fabric at each opening in box. Smooth fabric to inside of box at each opening.
4. Measure height of one side of box; add 2". Measure width of one side of box. Cut two pieces from fabric the determined measurement. Apply spray adhesive to wrong side of each fabric piece. Overlapping onto inside of box as necessary, center and smooth one fabric piece to each side of box.

5. Trace point pattern, page 154, onto tracing paper; cut out. Using pattern, cut fifteen points from fabric. Apply spray adhesive to wrong sides of points. Arrange and smooth five points around each opening in front of box.
6. For score numbers, apply desired numbers to front of box near openings.
7. For lid, measure width and length of opening at top of box; add 1" to each measurement. Use craft knife to cut a piece of cardboard the determined measurement. Cut a piece from fabric 1" larger on all sides than cardboard piece. Apply spray adhesive to wrong side of fabric piece. Overlapping onto back of cardboard piece as necessary, center and smooth fabric onto lid. Center and glue knob on lid. Place lid on box.
8. For each bean bag, cut two $3^{1}/_{2}$" squares from fabric. Matching wrong sides and leaving an opening for turning, use a $^{1}/_{4}$" seam allowance to sew squares together. Turn right side out. Fill bean bag with dried beans. Sew opening closed.

"Paws-itive" Comfort

*K*itty will love snuggling in for a long nap on this cozy bed that you can make from a cardboard box. Batting and a pillow provide a soft spot for your feline's napping comfort, and pretty fabric makes the bed decorative. Cover lids from spray paint cans with fabric for the legs, and glue on a nameplate displaying the name of the new owner.

KITTY BED

Recycled items: cardboard box and four lids from spray paint cans

You will also need a craft knife, cutting mat, tracing paper, batting, assorted fabrics, stapler, paper-backed fusible web, hot glue gun, decorative trim, $1^7/8$" dia. covered button kit, heavy-duty thread, purchased pillow to fit in bed, white acrylic paint, paintbrush, $1^1/2$" x $3^3/8$" frame charm, black permanent fine-point marker, and a $^7/8$" x $2^5/8$" piece of yellow card stock.

1. For foot and sides of bed, draw a line on one long and two short sides of box 3" from bottom. Use craft knife to cut out along drawn lines. Leaving 1" at sides and bottom, use craft knife to trim foot of bed (Fig. 1).

Fig. 1

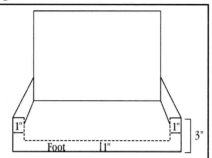

2. Draw around uncut side of box on tracing paper; cut out. Matching short edges, fold paper in half. For headboard pattern, referring to Fig. 2, and beginning 3" from bottom edges, draw a scallop design on paper. Cut out pattern along drawn lines. Unfold pattern. Aligning straight edge of pattern with inside bottom of box, draw around pattern on uncut side of box. Use craft knife to cut box along drawn lines.

Fig. 2

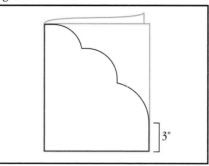

3. Cut one piece each from batting and fabric 15" larger on all sides than bottom of box. Center bottom of box on batting.

Trimming to fit and overlapping to inside, wrap batting around outside of box; staple to secure. Center bottom of box on wrong side of fabric. Trimming to fit and overlapping to inside, wrap fabric around outside of box; staple to secure.

4. Draw around headboard pattern on paper side of web. Fuse web to wrong side of fabric. Cutting $^1/4$" inside drawn line, cut out fabric piece. Cut a piece of batting $^1/4$" smaller on all sides than fabric piece. Glue batting piece to front of headboard. Covering batting, fuse fabric to front of headboard. Trimming to fit and covering raw edges, glue a length of trim around fused fabric piece.

5. For each leg, cut one 8" square each from batting and fabric. Gathering to fit and wrapping to inside as necessary, glue batting, then fabric to lid. Glue lids to bottom of bed at corners.

6. Follow manufacturer's instructions to cover button with fabric. Cut a 2" x 10" strip of fabric. Matching wrong sides and long edges, fold strip in half; press. Baste along long raw edges. Pull basting threads to gather strip. Gathering to fit around button, glue raw edges of strip around back of button.

7. For pillow accent, thread a needle with heavy-duty thread. Leaving a 5" tail and working from back of pillow, insert needle through center of pillow, then through covered button. Insert needle $^1/4$" away and back through pillow. Tie thread ends tightly at back of pillow to secure; trim ends. Place pillow in bed.

8. For nameplate, lightly paint frame charm white. Use marker to write pet's name on card stock piece. Insert card stock in frame. Glue nameplate to front of headboard.

"PURR-FECTLY" PLEASING

For a "purr-fectly" pleasing presentation, serve a special breakfast on this tray! To make it, just cover a cardboard box lid with wallpaper, then glue kitty greeting card motifs (or choose your own theme) to the inside of the tray. Spray with several coats of sealer to make the server durable, and add dressy ribbon handles.

DECOUPAGED TRAY

Recycled items: $3^1/_8$" x $11^1/_2$" x $17^3/_4$" cardboard box lid and greeting cards

You will also need spray adhesive, wallpaper, foam brush, decoupage glue, polyurethane spray sealer, 1"w ribbon, hot glue gun, and a stapler.

1. For tray, use spray adhesive to cover inside and outside of entire box lid with wallpaper.

2. Cut desired motifs from greeting cards. Use foam brush to apply glue to backs of motifs. Arrange and smooth motifs on bottom and inside sides of tray; allow to dry.

3. Apply two to three coats of sealer to bottom and inside sides of tray; allow to dry.

4. For handles, arrange and hot glue a 12" length of ribbon at each short end of tray. For stability, staple ends of ribbon to tray.

5. Trimming to fit and covering staples, hot glue ribbon around bottom edge of tray.

LET IT SHINE!

*B*righten up that boring corner *with our colorful stacked-box lamp! The simple patterns are painted on the assorted boxes and lampshade, creating a light with a whimsical charm all its own.*

BOX LAMP

Recycled items: 4" x 5³/₈" plastic container with lid, 2⁵/₈" x 5³/₄" x 5⁷/₈" cardboard box with lid, and a 3⁵/₈"h x 9¹/₄" dia. wooden container

You will also need white spray primer, lampshade, assorted colors of acrylic paint, paintbrushes, craft drill, hot glue gun, 20" long piece of medium-gauge craft wire, lamp kit, and desired color jumbo rickrack.

Allow primer and paint to dry after each application.

1. Remove lids from plastic container and box.
2. Apply primer to plastic container, plastic container lid, cardboard box, box lid, wooden container, and lampshade. Use acrylic paint to paint primed areas as desired.
3. Trimming to fit, glue rickrack around top and bottom of lampshade.

4. Drill ³/₈" dia. holes through center of plastic container lid, center of bottom of plastic container, center of box lid, center of bottom of box, center of bottom of wooden container, and ¹/₄" from top of wooden container on one side.
5. Replace lid on plastic container and on box. For lamp base, aligning holes, stack and glue plastic container on box, then box on wooden container.

6. Thread wire length down through holes in center of lamp base and out hole in side of wooden container. Wrap end of wire at side of wooden container around lamp cord. To thread lamp cord, carefully pull wire up through center of lamp base. Follow manufacturer's instructions to assemble lamp.

DESK DECOR

*A*dd *a floral flair to your desk with this elegant set! Simply decoupage a can and cardboard boxes with motifs cut from decorative napkins. Gluing wooden beads and finials to the boxes provides striking embellishments.*

BLUE-AND-WHITE DESK SET

Recycled items: two cardboard jewelry boxes with lids and a can
You will also need white spray primer, white spray paint, four 1" dia. wooden beads, two wooden finials, decorative paper napkins, spray adhesive, clear acrylic spray sealer, and a hot glue gun.

Allow primer, paint, and sealer to dry after each application.

1. Remove lids from boxes. Apply primer to outside of each box and lid and inside and outside of can. Spray paint boxes, lids, can, beads, and finials white.
2. Separate plies of napkins. Cut desired motifs from napkins. Apply spray adhesive to back of each motif. Position and smooth motifs onto boxes, lids, and can; allow to dry.
3. Apply two to three coats of sealer to boxes, lids, and can.
4. Hot glue beads to bottom corners of one box for feet. Center and hot glue one finial to each lid. Replace lids on boxes.

FEMININE FANCY

*D*on't toss that empty ice-cream tub — use it to create our charming wastebasket! Fashion a cover using pretty fabric and insert elastic in the casings to make it fit. Wrap up the fancy project with a wired-ribbon bow.

FABRIC-COVERED WASTEBASKET

Recycled item: 9³/₄" dia. x 10¹/₂"h cardboard container (we used a 3-gallon ice cream container)

You will also need ecru spray paint, 16" x 45" piece of fabric, safety pins, two 32" lengths of ¹/₄"w elastic, and 60" of 1¹/₂"w wired ribbon.

1. Spray paint inside of container; allow to dry.
2. Matching right sides, use a ¹/₄" seam allowance to sew short ends of fabric together to form a tube. For top casing, press one edge of tube ¹/₄", then 3¹/₂" to wrong side.
3. Leaving an opening at seam to insert elastic, sew along edge of first pressed edge. Sew ³/₄" from first pressed edge to form casing. Use safety pin to thread one length of elastic through casing. Sew ends

of elastic together. Sew opening in casing closed.
4. For bottom casing, press remaining raw edge of tube ¹/₄", then 1" to wrong

side. Repeat Step 3 to complete bottom casing.
5. Turn tube right side out. Place tube over container. Tie ribbon into a bow around top casing.

HOUSE "KEY-PER"

Having trouble keeping track of your keys? Then this homey key keeper is for you! Constructed using a cigar box, the house-shaped holder sports a shoe box roof and sponge-painted bricks. Assorted naturals provide the cottage-style landscaping.

CIGAR BOX KEY HOLDER

Recycled items: cigar box and a shoe box

You will also need a craft knife; cutting mat; foam core board; hot glue gun; ¹/₂"w masking tape; white spray primer; household sponge; tan acrylic paint; white, tan, and brown card stock; craft glue; black permanent fine-point marker; bronze dimensional paint; tracing paper; drawing compass; corrugated craft cardboard; assorted naturals (we used moss, leafy fronds, and dried white berries); small cup hooks; and a sawtooth picture hanger.

Refer to Painting Techniques, page 156, before beginning project. Use hot glue for all gluing unless otherwise indicated. Allow primer, paint, and craft glue to dry after each application.

1. Measure inside bottom width and length of cigar box. Use craft knife to cut two pieces of foam core board the determined measurements. Stack and glue foam core board pieces to inside bottom of cigar box.

2. Measure length of one short side of cigar box. Draw a line across one corner on bottom of shoe box the determined measurement (Fig. 1). Draw a second line 1" below first line.

Fig. 1

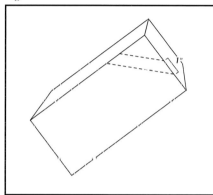

3. For housetop, use craft knife to cut along second drawn line and straight down sides of box. Referring to Fig. 2, make cuts along folded edges of housetop from cut edge to first drawn line. Folding along first drawn line and trimming excess cardboard at each corner to fit, fold flap to inside housetop at a 90° angle.

Fig. 2

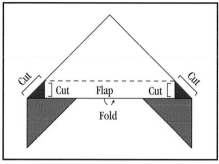

4. For siding, working from bottom edge to top and overlapping long edges, apply masking tape to front of housetop.

5. Glue housetop to one short end of cigar box. Trim edges of back of housetop even with back of cigar box.

6. For house, apply two to three coats of primer to inside and outside of cigar box and housetop. Cut a $^3/_4$" x $^7/_8$" piece from sponge. Sponge paint tan bricks on front and sides of house.

7. Cut four $1^1/_2$" x $2^1/_2$" pieces from white card stock for windows and sixteen $^1/_2$" x 1" pieces from tan card stock for panes. Arrange and use craft glue to glue panes to windows. Use craft glue to glue windows to house.

8. For door, cut one 2" x $4^1/_2$" piece from brown card stock. For door panels, cut two $^1/_2$" x $^3/_4$" pieces and two $^1/_2$" x $2^1/_4$" pieces from tan card stock. Arrange and use craft glue to glue panels to door. Use marker to outline panels. Use dimensional paint to add doorknob. Use craft glue to glue door to house.

9. Trace round window pattern, page 143, onto tracing paper. Draw around pattern on brown card stock; cut out shape. Use compass to draw a $1^1/_2$" dia. circle on tan card stock; cut out. Center and glue window over circle, then circle to housetop.

10. For roof panels, refer to Fig. 3 to measure width and height of roof; add $^1/_2$" to each measurement. Cut two pieces from cardboard the determined measurements. Bend one short end of each cardboard panel $^1/_2$" to uncorrugated side. Overlapping bends as necessary, glue roof panels to housetop.

Fig. 3

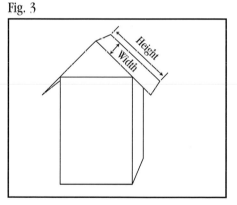

11. Arrange and glue naturals to house as desired. Screw cup hooks into foam core board inside house. Attach hanger to back of house.

HUNTER'S HIDEAWAY

*T*he hunter of the household will make good use of this storage box! Covered with camouflage fabric and embellished with pinecones and decorative trim, this container will help him keep track of all his necessities, from ammo to duck calls. What a great way to welcome hunting season!

CAMOUFLAGE BOX

Recycled items: shoe box with lid and large brown paper bags

You will also need two camouflage-print fabrics, ruler, spray adhesive, craft knife, cutting mat, cardboard, hot glue gun, wood-tone spray, decorative trim, assorted naturals to decorate box (we used bark, moss, and pinecones), and four 1" dia. wooden beads.

1. Remove lid from box.
2. Follow *Covering a Box*, page 159, to cover box with one fabric.
3. Measure width and length of bottom of box. Cut a piece from cardboard the determined measurements. Measure width and height of one end of box; add 1" to height measurement. Cut two pieces from cardboard the determined measurements. Measure width of one side of box; subtract $1/8$". Measure height of one side of box; add 1". Cut two pieces from cardboard the determined measurements.

4. For each cardboard piece, cut a piece from paper bag 1" larger on all sides than cardboard piece. Apply spray adhesive to wrong side of paper bag piece. Smoothing edges to back, smooth paper bag piece onto cardboard piece. Spot glue corners of paper bag piece to secure. Glue wrong side of cardboard pieces to bottom, ends, and sides of inside of box.
5. For lid, follow *Covering a Box*, page 159, to cover lid with remaining fabric.
6. Apply wood-tone spray to trim; allow to dry. Trimming to fit, glue a length of trim around edge of lid. Replace lid on box.
7. Arrange and glue naturals on side of box. Glue wooden beads to bottom corners of box for feet.

TASTEFUL TRINKET BOX

This beautiful bauble keeper started off as a cigar box and an ordinary greeting card. With our crafting know-how, you can display your own twice-treasured trinket box in no time at all!

TRINKET CIGAR BOX

Recycled items: cigar box and a floral-motif greeting card

You will also need red fabric, craft glue, hot glue gun, 3/8"w red gimp trim, red dimensional paint, 1/16" dia. red cord, 1/2" dia. red shank button, red acrylic paint, paintbrush, four 5/8" dia. x 3/4"h wooden spools, and four 5/8" dia. wooden cap buttons.

Allow craft glue and paint to dry after each application.

1. Measure width and length of cigar box lid; subtract 1/4" from each measurement. Cut a piece from fabric the determined measurements. Center and use craft glue to glue fabric piece to lid.
2. Trimming to fit, hot glue a length of trim around edges of fabric piece and around sides of box.
3. Cut desired motif from card. Center and use craft glue to glue motif to box lid.

Use dimensional paint to add details to motif.

4. For closure, cut a 3" length from cord. Hot glue ends of cord at center front edge of lid. Trimming to fit, hot glue a length of trim to lid around cord ends. Aligning button with closure, hot glue button to front side of box.

5. Paint spools and cap buttons red. For each leg, hot glue one cap button to one spool. Hot glue flat ends of legs to bottom corners of box.

129

BABY'S BOX

Baby's bath essentials will be close at hand in this decorative organizer — and who would have guessed that it began as a cheese container! We "babied" the box with batting, pastel fabrics, lace trim, decorative buttons, and bows.

BABY BOX ORGANIZER

Recycled item: 3³/₈" x 3³/₄" x 10³/₄" cardboard box

You will also need batting, hot glue gun, two coordinating fabrics, lightweight cardboard, spray adhesive, flat lace trim, assorted white buttons, and decorative bow trims.

1. Measure height of box. Measure around box. Cut two pieces from batting the determined measurements. Layer and glue each piece of batting around box.
2. Measure height of box; add 3". Measure around box; multiply by 2¹/₂. Piecing as necessary, cut a strip from seersucker fabric the determined measurements. Baste along each long edge of strip. Pull basting threads to gather strip to fit evenly around box. Overlapping ends at back and smoothing edges onto bottom and to inside of box, glue fabric strip around box.

3. Measure width and length of bottom of box. Rounding corners, cut a piece from cardboard the determined measurements. Cut a piece from seersucker fabric 1" larger on all sides than cardboard. Apply spray adhesive to wrong side of fabric piece. Smoothing edges to back, smooth fabric onto cardboard. Spot glue corners of fabric to secure. Glue fabric-covered cardboard to bottom of box.
4. Measure width and length of inside bottom of box. Cut a piece from cardboard the determined measurements. Cut a piece from print fabric 1" larger on all sides than cardboard. Apply spray adhesive to wrong side of fabric piece. Smoothing edges to back, smooth fabric onto cardboard. Spot glue corners of fabric to secure. Glue fabric-covered cardboard to inside bottom of box.
5. For inside side pieces, measure width and height of one inside side edge of box. Cut two pieces from cardboard the determined measurements. For inside end pieces, measure width and height of one inside end of box; subtract ¹/₈" from width measurement. Cut two pieces from cardboard the determined measurements. For each cardboard piece, cut a piece from print fabric 1" larger on all sides than cardboard piece. Apply spray adhesive to wrong side of fabric piece. Smoothing edges to back, smooth fabric onto cardboard. Spot glue corners of fabric to secure. Glue fabric-covered cardboard side pieces, then end pieces to inside of box.
6. Trimming to fit, glue lace around box. Arrange and glue buttons and bows to front of box.

CUSHY COMFORT

This stylish home accent is the perfect partner for a chair or sofa! An old pillow provides a padded top for a vegetable crate base, and batting makes the stool even cushier. Choose fabric that coordinates with your decor to cover the ottoman; then finish with ribbon accents at the corners.

VEGETABLE CRATE OTTOMAN

Recycled items: 12" x 12¹/₂" x 19" wooden vegetable crate with lid and a king-size pillow

You will also need batting, staple gun, fabrics, four 1¹/₂" dia. covered button kits, 5¹/₃ yds. of 1"w grosgrain ribbon, and a hot glue gun.

1. Measure from bottom front edge of crate, over top, to bottom back edge of crate; add 4". Measure width of top of crate. Cut two pieces from batting the determined measurements. Pulling batting taut and overlapping onto bottom of crate, wrap crate from front to back with batting pieces; staple to bottom of crate to secure.

2. Place pillow on top of crate; staple corners of pillow to crate to secure.

3. Measure from bottom of one side edge, over pillow, to bottom of remaining side edge of crate; add 4". Measure width of side of crate. Cut two pieces from batting the determined measurements. Pulling batting taut and overlapping onto bottom of crate, wrap crate from side to side with batting pieces; staple to bottom of crate to secure.

4. Measure from bottom front edge of crate, over pillow, to bottom back edge of crate; add 4". Measure from bottom of one side edge, over pillow, to bottom of remaining side edge of crate; add 4". Cut a piece from fabric the determined

measurements. Pulling fabric taut, overlapping onto bottom of crate, and gathering excess at corners, wrap crate with fabric; staple to bottom of crate to secure.

5. For each accent, follow manufacturer's instructions to cover one button with fabric. Cut four 6" lengths from ribbon. Matching short ends, fold each ribbon length in half to form loops; glue ends to secure. Cut two 12" lengths from ribbon for streamers. Arrange and glue loops, then streamers to back of fabric-covered button. Glue one accent to gathers at each corner of ottoman.

COTTAGE GARDEN TOTE

A *true gardener is always prepared — and a handy garden tote fashioned from a detergent box will help keep things organized! Cut motifs from magazines and decoupage them to the box to make a garden scene. A trim of ivy garland around the handle is the perfect finale.*

GARDEN TOTE BOX

Recycled items: large detergent box with plastic handle and magazines
You will also need a craft knife, cutting mat, grey spray primer, grey acrylic paint, paintbrush, foam brush, decoupage glue, clear acrylic spray sealer, medium-gauge craft wire, wire cutters, and an artificial ivy garland.

Allow primer, paint, and sealer to dry after each application.

1. Use craft knife to cut top from box.
2. Apply primer to box. Paint box grey.
3. Cut desired motifs from magazines. Use foam brush to apply decoupage glue to backs of motifs. Arrange and smooth motifs on box; allow to dry.
4. Apply two to three coats of sealer to box.
5. Use wire to attach garland along handle.

GARDEN GATE SIGN
(page 70)

little by little

day by day

friends & f(l)owers

grow that way

PRINCESS ROOM SIGN
(page 13)

POP-UP PUPPET
(page 17)

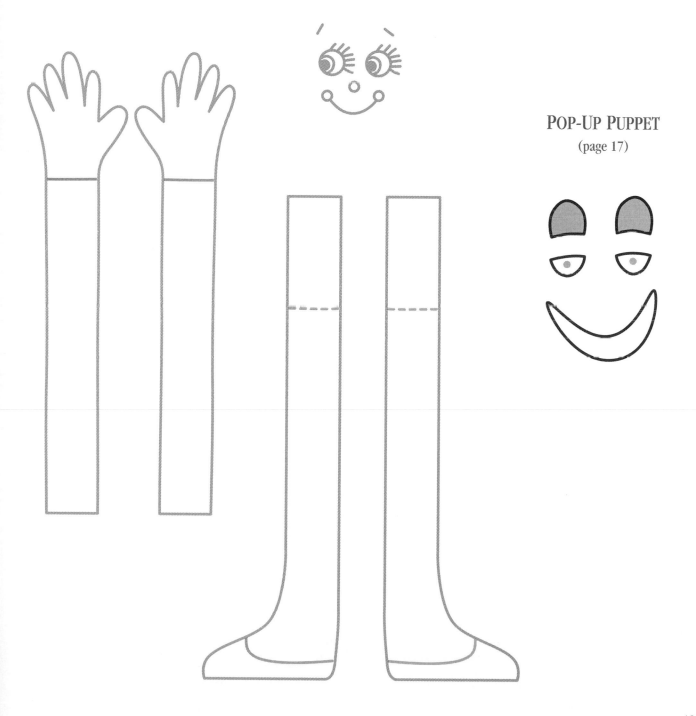

135

HOLIDAY PAPER BAG ORNAMENTS
(page 42)

HOLIDAY PAPER BAG ORNAMENTS (continued)

CAN MAN FOUNTAIN
(page 26)

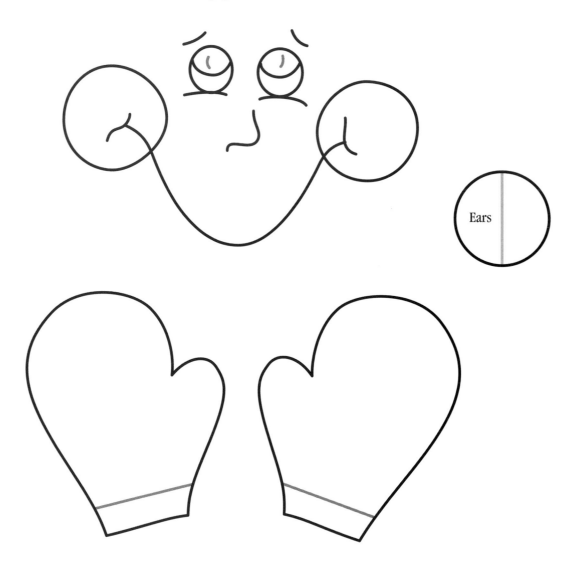

Ears

How does your Garden grow?

PATTERNS (continued)

LADYBUG BIRDHOUSE
(page 10)

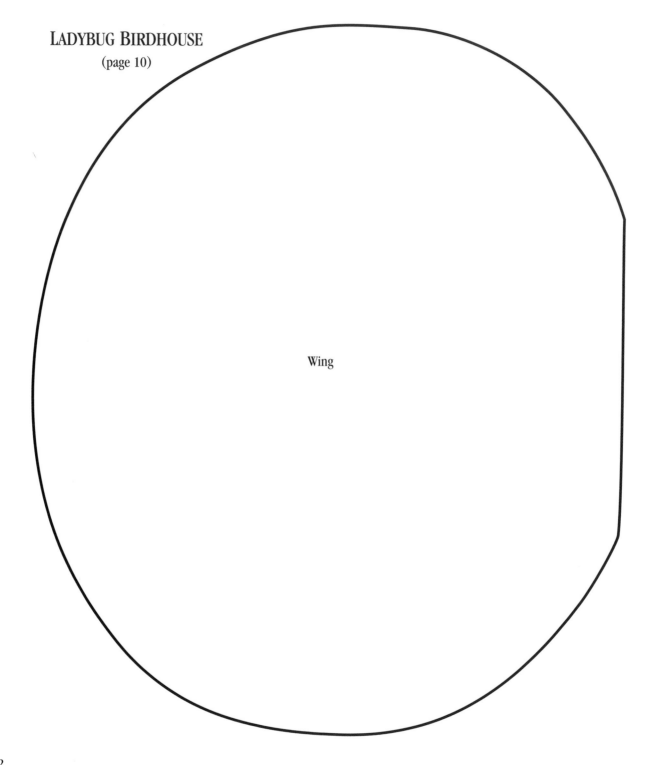

Wing

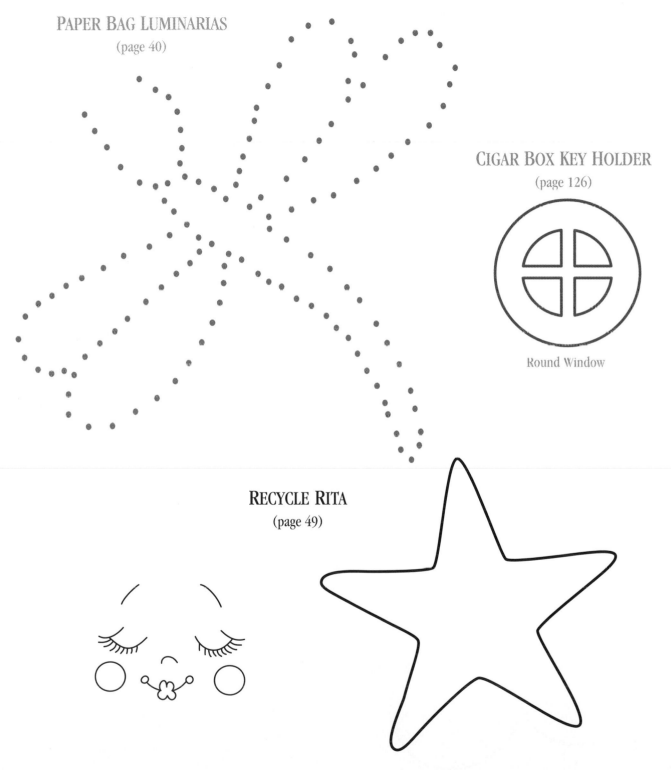

PAPER BAG LUMINARIAS
(page 40)

CIGAR BOX KEY HOLDER
(page 126)

Round Window

RECYCLE RITA
(page 49)

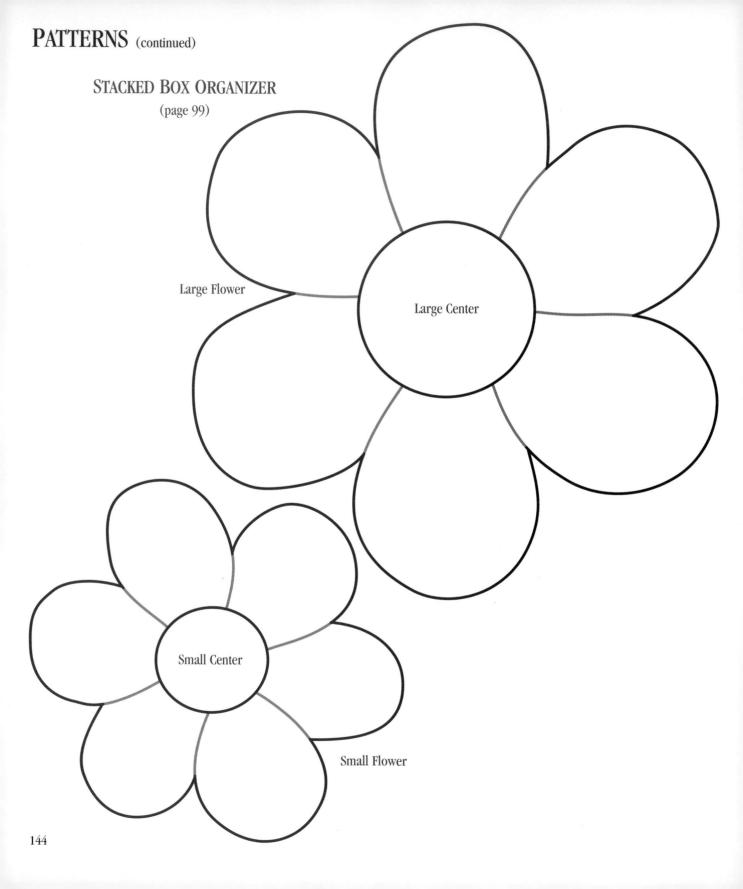

PATTERNS (continued)

STACKED BOX ORGANIZER
(page 99)

Large Flower

Large Center

Small Center

Small Flower

ART SUPPLY CONTAINER
(page 15)

HOBBY HORSE
(page 86)

Mouth

BUG-TOP CANISTERS
(page 20)

Wings

Eye

Ear

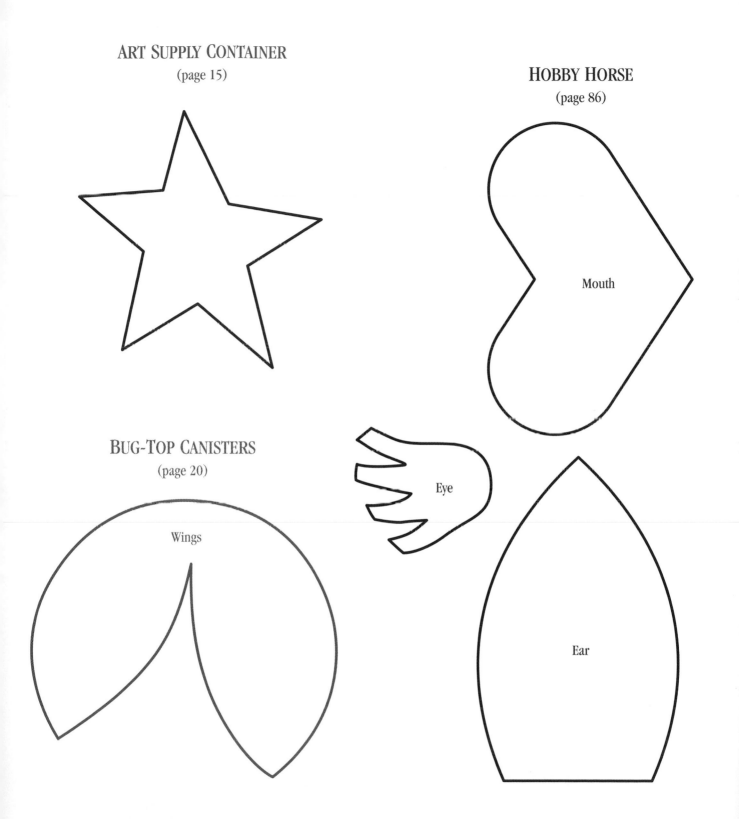

PATTERNS (continued)

Comb

Wing

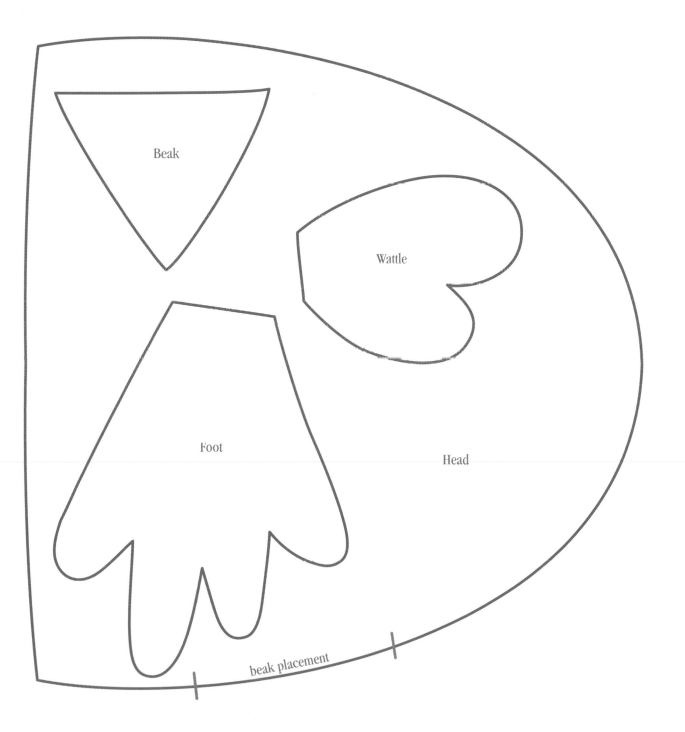

Beak

Wattle

Foot

Head

beak placement

PATTERNS (continued)

BEADED PAPER BAG JEWELRY
(page 41)

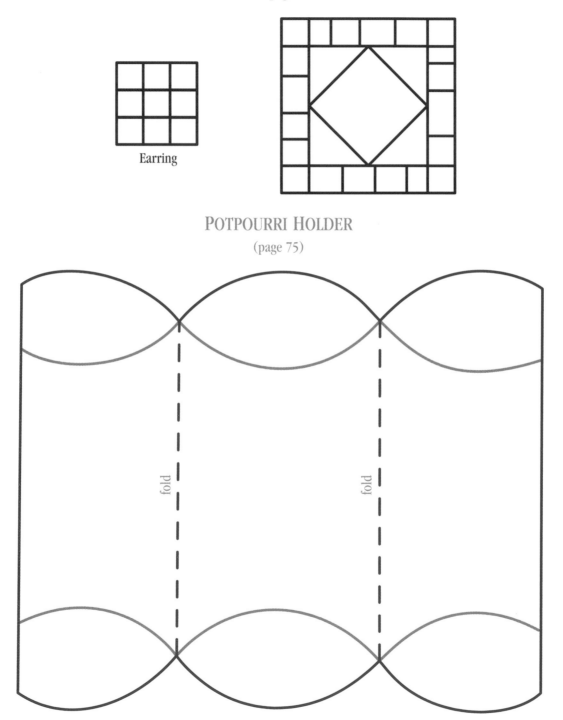

Earring

POTPOURRI HOLDER
(page 75)

fold

fold

STUFFED ANIMAL CADDY
(page 87)

WALL HANGING
(page 45)

PANSY WREATH

(page 44)

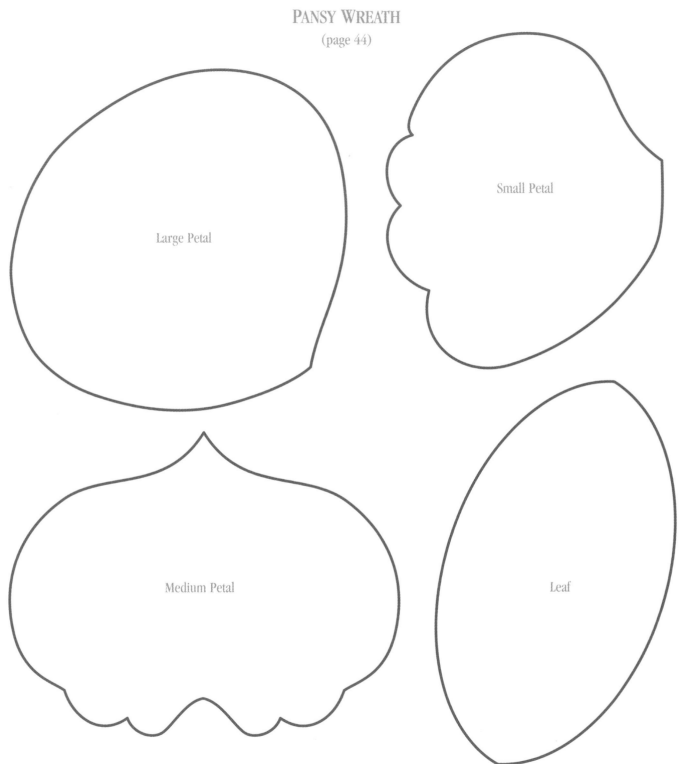

Large Petal

Small Petal

Medium Petal

Leaf

PLAY BACKPACK
(page 43)

PINCUSHION
(page 84)

HANGING CAN CANDLE HOLDERS
(page 31)

SOCK DRAFT DODGER
(page 83)

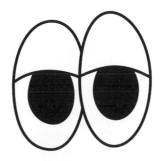

PATTERNS (continued)

SOCK PINS
(page 90)

GIFT HOLDERS
(page 21)

Leisure Arts, Inc., grants permission to the owner of this book to photocopy the label design on this page for personal use only.

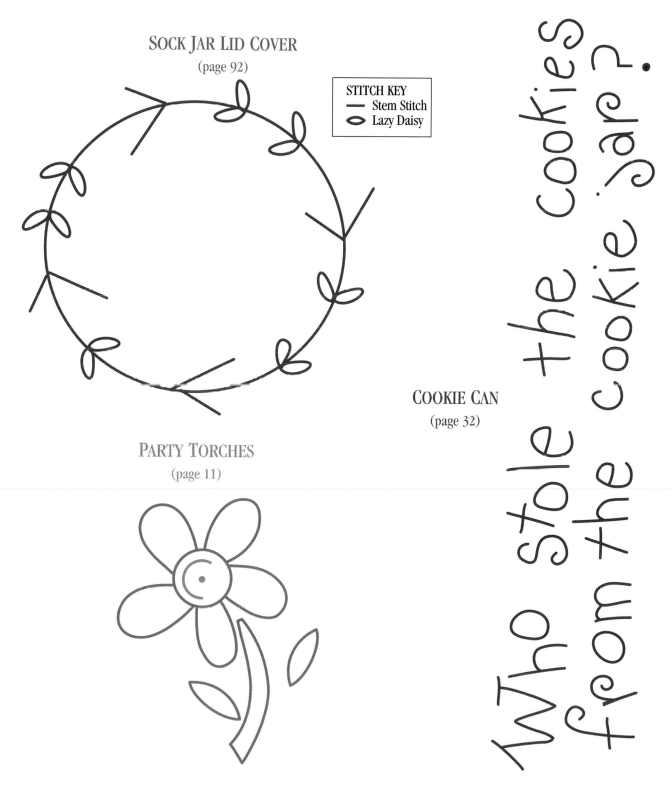

SOCK JAR LID COVER
(page 92)

STITCH KEY
— Stem Stitch
⬮ Lazy Daisy

COOKIE CAN
(page 32)

PARTY TORCHES
(page 11)

Who stole the cookies from the cookie jar?

PATTERNS (continued)

DOGGIE WINDOW TREATMENT
(page 82)

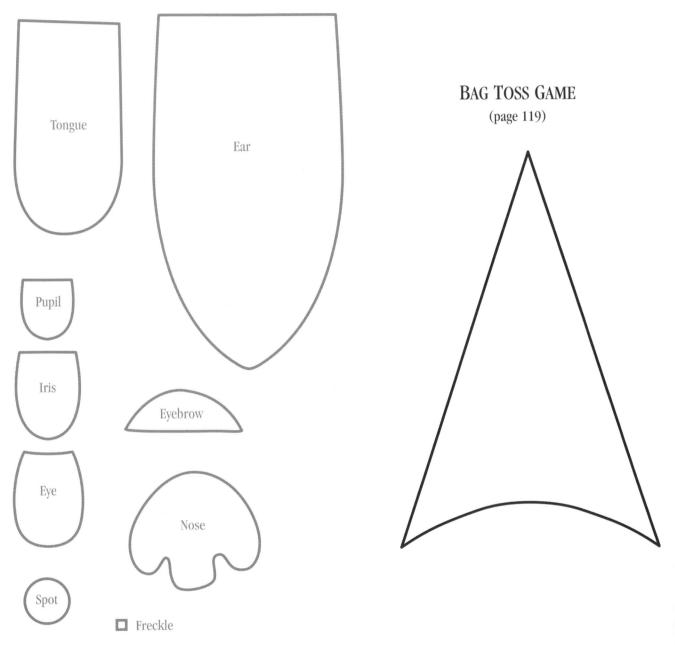

Tongue

Ear

Pupil

Iris

Eyebrow

Eye

Nose

Spot

☐ Freckle

BAG TOSS GAME
(page 119)

LOONY BIRD

(page 23)

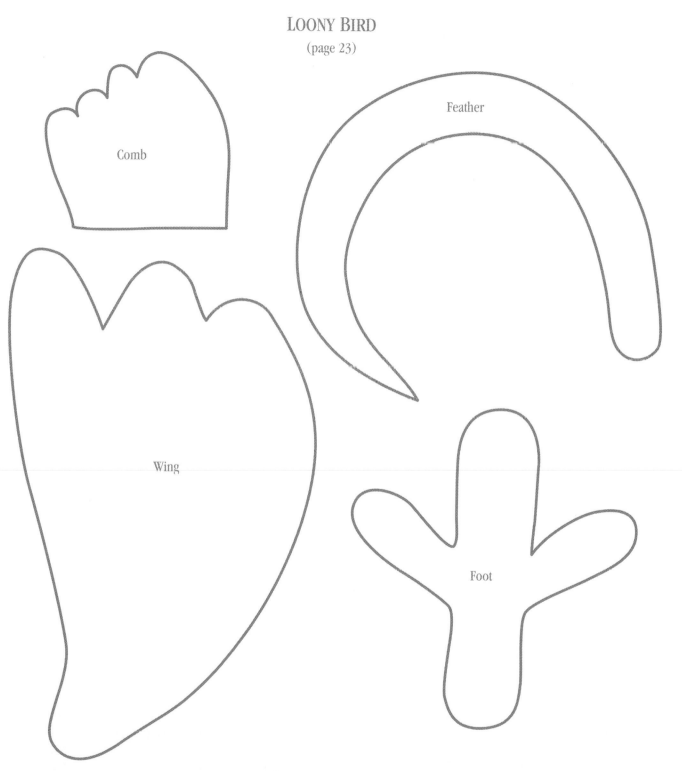

Comb

Feather

Wing

Foot

GENERAL INSTRUCTIONS

ADHESIVES

When using any adhesive, carefully follow the manufacturer's instructions.

White craft glue: Recommended for paper. Dry flat.

Tacky craft glue: Recommended for paper, fabric, floral, or wood. Dry flat or secure items with clothespins or straight pins until glue is dry.

Craft glue stick: Recommended for paper or for gluing small, lightweight items to paper or other surface. Dry flat.

Fabric glue: Recommended for fabric or paper. Dry flat or secure items with clothespins or straight pins until glue is dry.

Decoupage glue: Recommended for decoupaging fabric or paper to a surface such as wood or glass. Use purchased decoupage glue or mix one part craft glue with one part water.

Hot or low-temperature glue gun: Recommended for paper, fabric, floral, or wood. Hold in place until set.

Rubber cement: Recommended for paper and cardboard. May discolor photos; may discolor paper with age. Dry flat (dries very quickly).

Spray adhesive: Recommended for paper or fabric. Can be repositionable or permanent. Dry flat.

Household Cement: Recommended for ceramic or metal. Secure items with clothespins until glue is dry.

Wood Glue: Recommended for wood. Nail, screw, or clamp items together until glue is dry.

COFFEE DYEING

1. Dissolve two tablespoons instant coffee in two cups hot water; allow to cool.
2. Soak fabric pieces in coffee several minutes. Remove from coffee and allow to dry; press.

TEA DYEING

1. Steep one tea bag in two cups hot water; allow to cool. Remove tea bag.
2. Soak fabric pieces in tea until desired color is achieved. Remove from tea and allow to dry; press.

MAKING PATTERNS

For a more durable pattern, use a permanent pen to trace pattern onto stencil plastic.

Place tracing paper over pattern and trace pattern; cut out.

PAINTING TECHNIQUES

TRANSFERRING A PATTERN

Trace pattern onto tracing paper. Place transfer paper coated side down between project and traced pattern. Use removable tape to secure pattern to project. Use a pencil to transfer outlines of design to project (press lightly to avoid smudges and heavy lines that are difficult to cover). If necessary, use a soft eraser to remove any smudges.

PAINTING BASE COATS

A disposable foam plate makes a good palette.

Use a medium round brush for large areas and a small round brush for small areas. Do not overload brush. Allowing to dry between coats, apply several thin coats of paint to project.

TRANSFERRING DETAILS

To transfer detail lines to design, reposition pattern and transfer paper over painted base coats and use a pencil to lightly transfer detail lines onto project.

ADDING DETAILS

Use a permanent pen to draw over detail lines.

DIMENSIONAL PAINT

Before painting on project, practice painting on scrap fabric or paper.

1. To keep paint flowing smoothly, turn bottle upside down and allow paint to fill tip of bottle before each use.
2. Clean tip often with a paper towel.
3. If tip becomes clogged, insert a straight pin into tip opening.
4. When painting lines or painting over appliqués, keep bottle tip in contact with surface of project, applying a line of paint centered over drawn line or raw edge of appliqué.
5. To correct a mistake, use a paring knife to gently scrape excess paint from project before it dries. Carefully remove stain with non-acetone nail polish remover. A mistake may also be camouflaged by incorporating the mistake into the design.
6. Lay project flat for 24 hours to ensure that paint has set.

SPONGE PAINTING

1. Dampen sponge with water.
2. Dip dampened sponge into paint; blot on paper towel to remove excess paint.
3. Use a light stamping motion to paint project.

SPATTER PAINTING

1. Place item on flat surface.
2. Mix one part paint with one part water. Dip toothbrush in diluted paint and pull thumb firmly across bristles to spatter paint on item. Repeat until desired effect is achieved. Allow to dry.

ANTIQUING

"Antiquing" can be applied to bare wood, over paint, or over a clear finish. Test this technique on an inconspicuous area of the item you are antiquing to ensure desired results.

For stain, use brown waterbase stain or mix one part brown acrylic paint with one part water. Working on one small area at a time, use foam brush to apply stain to item; blot or wipe immediately with a soft cloth to remove excess stain. Allow to dry. Repeat as desired for darker antiquing.

MAKING APPLIQUÉS

To prevent darker fabrics from showing through, white or light-colored fabrics may need to be lined with fusible interfacing before applying paper-backed fusible web.

Follow all steps for each appliqué. When tracing patterns for more than one appliqué, leave at least 1" between shapes on web.

To make a reverse appliqué piece, trace pattern onto tracing paper; turn traced pattern over and continue to follow all steps using reversed pattern.

When an appliqué pattern contains shaded areas, trace along entire outer line for appliqué indicated in project instructions. Trace outer lines of shaded areas separately for additional appliqués indicated in project instructions.

Appliqués can be temporarily held in place by touching appliqués with tip of iron. If appliqués are not in desired position, lift and reposition.

1. Use a pencil to trace pattern onto paper side of web as many times as indicated in project instructions for a single fabric. Repeat for additional patterns and fabrics.
2. Follow manufacturer's instructions to fuse traced patterns to wrong side of fabrics. Do not remove paper backing.
3. Cut out appliqué pieces along traced lines. Remove paper backing.
4. Overlapping as necessary, arrange appliqués web side down on project.
5. Fuse appliqués in place.

MACHINE APPLIQUÉ

Unless otherwise indicated in project instructions, set sewing machine for a medium-width zigzag stitch with a short stitch length. When using nylon or metallic thread, use regular thread in bobbin.

1. Pin or baste a piece of stabilizer slightly larger than design to wrong side of background fabric under design.
2. Beginning on straight edge of appliqué if possible, position project under presser foot so that most of stitching will be on appliqué piece. Hold upper thread toward you and sew two or three stitches over thread to prevent raveling. Stitch over all exposed raw edges of appliqué and along detail lines as indicated in project instructions.
3. When stitching is complete, remove stabilizer. Pull loose threads to wrong side of fabric; knot and trim ends.

GENERAL INSTRUCTIONS (continued)

EMBROIDERY STITCHES

BACKSTITCH

Bring needle up at 1; go down at 2. Bring needle up at 3 and back down at 1 (Fig. 1). Continue working to make a continuous line of stitches.

Fig. 1

BLANKET STITCH

Bring needle up at 1; keeping thread below point of needle, go down at 2 and up at 3 (Fig. 2a). Continue working as shown in Fig. 2b.

Fig. 2a   Fig. 2b

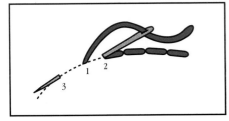

CROSS STITCH

Bring needle up at 1 and go down at 2. Come up at 3 and go down at 4 (Fig. 3).

Fig. 3

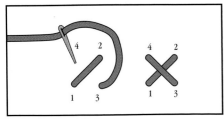

FRENCH KNOT

Bring needle up at 1. Wrap floss once around needle and insert needle at 2, holding floss with non-stitching fingers (Fig. 4). Tighten knot as close to fabric as possible while pulling needle back through fabric. For larger knot, use more strands of floss; wrap only once.

Fig. 4

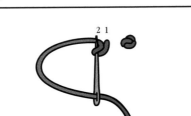

LAZY DAISY

Bring needle up at 1 and go down at 2 to form a loop; bring needle up at 3, keeping thread below point of needle (Fig. 5a). Go down at 4 to anchor loop (Fig. 5b).

Fig. 5a   Fig. 5b

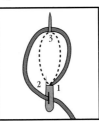

RUNNING STITCH

Make a series of straight stitches with stitch length equal to the space between stitches (Fig. 6).

Fig. 6

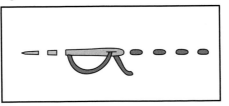

STEM STITCH

Bring needle up at 1. Keeping thread below stitching line, go down at 2 and up at 3. Go down at 4 and up at 5 (Fig. 7).

Fig. 7

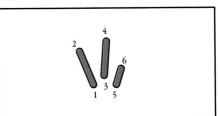

STRAIGHT STITCH

Bring needle up at 1 and go down at 2 (Fig. 8). Length of stitches may be varied as desired.

Fig. 8

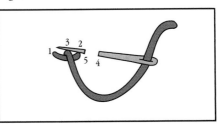

COVERING A LAMPSHADE

1. To make pattern, find seamline of lampshade. If shade does not have a seamline, draw a vertical line from top edge to bottom edge of shade.
2. Centering tissue paper edge on shade seamline, tape in place. Wrap paper around shade, extending 1" past seamline; tape to secure (Fig. 1).

Fig. 1

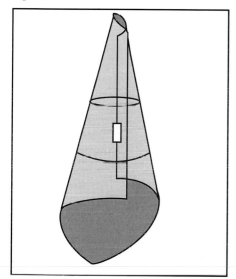

3. Trace along top and bottom edges of shade. Draw a vertical line from top edge to bottom edge of shade 1" past seamline. Remove paper; cut along drawn lines.
4. Use pattern to cut cover from desired fabric or paper.
5. Fold one straight edge of covering 1/2" to wrong side; press.
6. Matching unpressed straight edge of covering to seamline, use spray adhesive to apply covering to shade. Use glue to secure pressed edge.

COVERING A BOX

1. Cut a piece of paper or fabric large enough to cover box. Center box or fabric on wrong side of paper and draw around box.
2. Use ruler to draw lines 1/2" outside drawn lines, extending lines to edges of paper. Draw diagonal lines from intersections of outer lines to corners of original lines.
3. Cut away corners of paper and clip along diagonal lines (Fig. 1).

Fig. 1

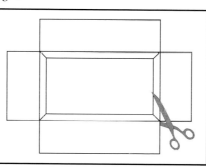

4. Apply spray adhesive to wrong side of paper.
5. Center box on paper, matching box to original drawn lines; smooth paper on bottom of box.
6. To cover front and back of box, smooth paper onto front and back sides of box. Smooth excess paper around corners onto adjacent sides. Smooth paper to inside of box, clipping as necessary (Fig. 2).

Fig. 2

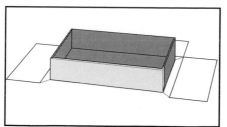

7. To cover each end, smooth paper onto end of box. Use craft knife and ruler to trim excess paper even with corners. Smooth paper to inside of box.

CUTTING A FABRIC CIRCLE

1. Cut a square of fabric the size indicated in project instructions.
2. Matching right sides, fold fabric square in half from top to bottom and again from left to right.
3. Tie one end of a length of string to a pencil. Measuring from pencil, insert a thumbtack through string at length indicated in project instructions. Insert thumbtack through folded corner of fabric. Holding tack in place and keeping string taut, mark cutting line (Fig. 1).

Fig. 1

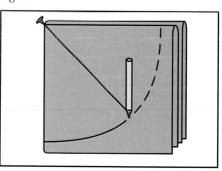

4. For additional cutting lines, repeat Step 3.
5. Cut along drawn lines through all fabric layers.

CREDITS

We want to extend a warm *thank you* to the generous people who allowed us to photograph our projects at their homes: Sandra Cook, Jodie Davis, Stacy Grundfest, Virginia Hickingbotham, Ellison Poe, Duncan and Nancy Porter, Molly Satterfield, Leighton Weeks, and Nancy Zuerlein.

To Wisconsin Technicolor LLC of Pewaukee, Wisconsin, we say thank you for the superb color reproduction and excellent pre-press preparation.

We especially want to thank photographers Mark Mathews, Larry Pennington, and Ken West of Peerless Photography, and Jerry R. Davis of Jerry Davis Photography, all of Little Rock, Arkansas, for their time, patience, and excellent work.

Thanks also go to Ruth Ann Epperson, who assisted in testing the projects in this book.